COMPASSION, MORALITY
AND THE MEDIA

ISSUES in CULTURAL and MEDIA STUDIES

Series editor: Stuart Allan

COMPASSION, MORALITY AND THE MEDIA

Keith Tester

OPEN UNIVERSITY PRESS
Buckingham · Philadelphia

Open University Press
Celtic Court
22 Ballmoor
Buckingham
MK18 1XW

email: enquiries@openup.co.uk
world wide web: www.openup.co.uk

and
325 Chestnut Street
Philadelphia, PA 19106, USA

First Published 2001

A catalogue record of this book is available from the British Library

ISBN 0 335 20513 5 (pb)   0 335 20514 3 (hb)

Library of Congress Cataloging-in-Publication Data
Tester, Keith, 1960–
    Compassion, morality, and the media/Keith Tester.
        p.   cm. – (Issues in cultural and media studies)
    Includes bibliographical references and index.
    ISBN 0-335-20514-3 – ISBN 0-335-20513-5 (pbk.)
    1. Mass media – Moral and ethical aspects.   2. Sympathy.   I. Title
    II. Series.

P94.T44 2001
175–dc21   00-060650

Typeset by Type Study, Scarborough
Printed in Great Britain by Biddles Limited, Guildford and Kings Lynn

CONTENTS

SERIES EDITOR'S FOREWORD

Writing in the *London Review of Books* at the time of the Falkland/Malvinas Islands conflict, Raymond Williams argued that underlying the familiar issues which arise when news reports are being examined, such as 'issues of control and independence; of the quality of reporting; of access and balance in discussion,' was a deeper problematic. In order to describe it, he coined the phrase 'the culture of distance'. Reminding us that the televisual picture of the world is, of course, a selective one, he pointed out that 'what is much more significant is the revealed distance between the technology of television, as professionally understood, managed and interpreted, and the political and cultural space within which it actually operates'. It is across this distance, he observed, that the tragic devastation endemic to warfare is recurrently taken-up and re-inflected by television news into an 'antiseptic' presentation of reality. Hence his urgent call for new investigations to be made into this culture of distance, this 'latent culture of alienation, within which men and women are reduced to models, figures and the quick cry in the throat'.

In the spirit of this type of intervention, Keith Tester's *Compassion, Morality and the Media* constitutes an important engagement with current debates about the ethical implications engendered by media portrayals of the distant suffering of others. It takes as its point of departure into these debates the issue of 'compassion fatigue', a modern syndrome frequently attributed to media audiences ostensibly overwhelmed by the sheer volume of reports concerning human tragedies from around the globe. The cumulative effects of such reports, it is claimed, work to psychologically numb audience members into ceasing to care anymore, thereby undermining their capacity to get involved and lend assistance. Tester proceeds to unravel the precepts informing this compassion fatigue thesis, firstly through a careful explication of the relevant kinds of ethical judgements being made routinely by journalists. Next, his attention turns to the audience members themselves, where he suggests that 'compassion is only identifiable as morality as and when it is the basis of distinctive forms of social action on the part of the actors who together constitute the audience'. Subsequent chapters elaborate upon this line of enquiry into the 'moral horizons of audiences', exploring related topics as diverse as the photographs used in charitable appeals, the impact of 24 hour rolling news or the so-called 'CNN Effect', and broadcast telethons, amongst others. In each instance, Tester shows that however bored and apathetic we might be at times, sometimes something happens which 'stirs us out of stupor and inspires us to take part in events'. Examining the complexities, and lived contradictions, of compassion is thus shown to be of vital significance for furthering our understanding of the everyday experience of media culture.

The Issues in Cultural and Media Studies series aims to facilitate a diverse range of critical investigations into pressing questions considered to be central to current thinking and research. In light of the remarkable speed at which the conceptual agendas of cultural and media studies are changing, the authors are committed to contributing to what is an ongoing process of re-evaluation and critique. Each of the books is intended to provide a lively, innovative and comprehensive introduction to a specific topical issue from a fresh perspective. The reader is offered a thorough grounding in the most salient debates indicative of the book's subject, as well as important insights into how new modes of enquiry may be established for future explorations. Taken as a whole, then, the series is designed to cover the core components of cultural and media studies courses in an imaginatively distinctive and engaging manner.

Stuart Allan

INTRODUCTION

We have all had the experience of reading a newspaper or watching the television and of being deeply moved by some of the horrors we read about or see, some of the **suffering** and misery which other people are forced to experience through no fault of their own. Why do these **reports** and **representations** move us? How do they move us? And what are we likely to do about it? Do you feel upset when you see a tortured baby? Do you shrug without a care and blame them for living in such stupid places when you read or hear about flood victims in Africa? Do you think that some people are simply fated to suffer and that there is nothing to be done about it? Do you take part in **telethon** appeals? Why?

These are the questions which this book seeks to explore and examine.

It seems to me to be curious that although we all watch television and read newspapers (or at least, the vast majority of us do those things), and although we are all therefore aware of the problem of what the suffering on the screen or the page might mean to us, this whole series of questions has received virtually no sustained academic attention. There are a few books and articles which are relevant to the matter but, so far as I can discover, nothing that deals with the problem of the suffering and misery of distant **others** in anything approaching a developed and focused way. The honourable exception is Luc Boltanski's *Distant Suffering: Morality, Media and Politics* (Boltanski 1999). I would hope that anyone who wishes to pursue the debates which are raised in this book (if only to take issue with them) will pay Boltanski's book the serious attention it deserves.

The book feels its way into the question of the moral **compulsion** of the media through a detailed consideration of the theme of **compassion fatigue**.

A very short Chapter 1 seeks to establish parameters within which it is possible for us to think about all of these issues, by comparing and contrasting the arguments of social thinkers on the one hand and journalists on the other. Chapters 2 and 3 concentrate on different aspects of the compassion fatigue issue; Chapter 2 on compassion fatigue and journalistic production and Chapter 3 on compassion fatigue and the **moral** horizons of the **audience**. In particular, Chapter 3 examines the possibility that men and women might experience **compassion** in very different ways. Meanwhile, Chapters 4 and 5 follow through on the widespread belief that there is nothing we can do about all the suffering and misery in the world. The interesting point is that the people who say that there is nothing to be done are also likely to get involved in telethon appeals in order to do something. In other words, there seems to be a gap between what people think and what they do. Chapter 4 examines how media texts might spur the compassion of the audience and Chapter 5 looks at the kinds of **moral action** that might ensue.

I ought to make it clear that throughout the discussion I am not seeking to 'take sides' in the debate about whether or not compassion fatigue actually 'exists'. Although my own views on compassion will probably become clear as the book proceeds, and although I think that the whole debate about compassion fatigue has a number of significant logical problems (not least: what is the 'normal' level of compassion that is presumably being fatigued?), I use compassion fatigue as a way into a series of debates rather than as something to be analysed on its own terms. That is why I frequently refer to the compassion fatigue *thesis*.

I hope that this is a book that will be used as a kind of invitation to a series of possible debates rather than as the statement of a position. This is a book of questions, not answers. The answers are for you to provide. I hope that this book will be treated as a source of themes and debates to be explored and assessed by reference to the coverage of the ever lengthening catalogue of the misery of the people of the world. I hope that this book will be used as a partner with which to think and work. It should not be treated as a text merely to be read.

In order to encourage you to work with this book, and to construct its relevance for yourself, I have chosen not to include pictures or a lot of background information about some of the incidents to which I refer. This is for a couple of reasons. First, I have always thought that one sure way of making a book date really quickly is to include photographs which are amazingly contemporary when the text is sent to the publisher and astonishingly old hat when the book finally appears. This problem also surrounds historical events; what seems to me to be important today might not seem to be so pressing tomorrow. In any case, if I have referred to a historical event which continues to be pressing but is shrouded in mystery, that forgetting of the circumstances of its emergence (and instead its 'naturalization') is precisely one of the questions which the book wants to examine. Second, I have not included pictures because, as I said before, I would like this to be a book which is used and, therefore, I think it is more valuable for everyone if you gather illustrative material for yourself, in terms of your own media reading and viewing, in terms of your own feelings of compassion.

I would like to thank Stuart Allan and Justin Vaughan for thinking that I was up to the task of writing this book. I hope I have gone some little way towards repaying their trust. I would also like to thank Linda Rutherford and Madeleine Tester, Jo Mooney and Graham Spencer for their help. I am to blame for everything between these covers.

PARAMETERS FOR A DEBATE

1

Introduction

It is useful to set up the parameters within which the rest of this book will operate. This can be achieved if we spend a little time considering two different approaches to the issue and the question of how the media might – or might not – be morally compelling. The first parameter can be established by a couple of theoretical statements about the moral compulsion of the media. These are statements which can be found in the work of two of the most sophisticated social thinkers of the present, Alain Finkielkraut and Zygmunt Bauman. The second parameter is provided by statements which have been made by a couple of journalists reflecting on the moral relevance of their profession and, perhaps more interestingly, the gap between what they intended the audience to see and hear and what the audience evidently did see and hear.

Theoretical insights

In what is, admittedly, a slightly obscure reference (a footnote to the main text of his denunciation of Holocaust revisionism), the French philosopher Alain Finkielkraut writes that when it comes to the problem of world hunger, we are in a different situation from our ancestors because we do not have the defence of ignorance. Whereas our ancestors could claim, probably in all good conscience, that they did nothing about famine in Africa or slaughter in Asia because they knew nothing about it, we cannot develop that kind of argument without lying to ourselves. We know, we know we know and everybody else knows that we know (this is a problem which is dealt with in the context of Western responses to the war in the Balkans in Cushman and Mestrovic 1996).

For Finkielkraut, 'public indifference can no longer be attributed to *ignorance* as it once could' (Finkielkraut 1998: 141). This means that it is impossible to uphold ideals about the essential moral goodness of humanity and of individual people. After all, if we were good and kindly as some Enlightenment moral narratives suggest, we would not be able to know about the famines with such equanimity. But we do know and we do not feel ourselves to be overly stirred into **action**. Consequently, Finkielkraut felt that it was appropriate to make the general statement that, 'The more suffering that people see on their TV screens, the less concerned they feel. Current events demobilize them; images kill the feeling of obligation within them'. He went on to claim that, 'The public is blasé: news reports fail to take their audience beyond the realm of everyday experience, and they insinuate the most monstrous realities into the everyday by marking them with the stamp of deja-vu' (Finkielkraut 1998: 141). In all, Finkielkraut believes that, 'public indifference is now the result of habit' and that, 'In order to *break public opinion of this habit*, one is almost naturally led to up the ante. Famine attains the status of genocide, and the West's *responsibility* for the Third World's delayed development becomes the West's *extermination* of Third World peoples' (Finkielkraut 1998: 141, original emphasis. Finkielkraut's book was originally published in France in 1982. It is therefore worth reading alongside some of the points that are made in Baudrillard 1994. Baudrillard's book was first published in France in 1992).

A comparable position has been hinted at by Zygmunt Bauman in a couple of sentences that are not really developed in his book *Postmodern Ethics* (Bauman 1993). There, he mentions an idea of the *telecity* which draws on the Simmelian theme of the status of the stranger in the modern metropolis (see the essay on 'The Stranger' in Simmel 1950). According to Simmel, of course, the stranger who is perpetually encountered in the spaces and places of the metropolis tends to be dealt with through strategies of avoidance and disengagement. For Simmel, precisely because the stranger is unknown, the individual attempts to make sense of this mysterious presence by a turning away from social relationships. Bauman follows this lead when he says that strangers are now also represented by television and that yet, in that representation, they lose their embodied presence and in so doing they lose their moral integrity. They become something other than fully and experientially properly human. He says that, 'The strangers (the surfaces of strangers) whom the televiewer confronts are "telemediated". There is, comfortingly, a glass screen to which their lives are confined'. Bauman goes on: 'the reduction of their existential mode to pure *surface* is now, at long last, tangibly obvious, indubitable, technologically guaranteed' (Bauman 1993: 177–8). Television thus achieves what the city could not. Whereas the stranger in the city retains and remains a physical and material presence, according to Bauman the stranger in the telecity is flattened out so that her or his presence to the viewer is without any great substance.

It is clear from the tone of the passages from Bauman that, for him, the telecity (the television as the agent of the imagination of a universal city of strangers) is of enormous consequence for moral relationships and ties between the viewers and the people on the screen. This is obvious from his comment about strangers become surfaces. The inhabitants of his telecity are disembodied and disindividuated; instead they are aestheticized (they are represented as surfaces) that are denied a moral compulsion precisely because they lack any deep integrity or objectivity. For Bauman then, the telecity symbolizes the replacement of the moral by the aesthetic to such an extent that it becomes reasonable to question whether it remains valid to talk about morality in this particular field.

But when he reaches that kind of conclusion, Bauman turns the debate about the compulsion of television for moral relationships to the discourse of pleasure. As he puts it: 'In the telecity, the others appear solely as objects of enjoyment, no strings attached . . . Offering amusement is their only right to exist – and a right which it is up to them to confirm ever anew, with each successive "switching on" ' (Bauman 1993: 178). As such, even though Bauman gestures towards crucially important themes and concerns, his own treatment of the relationship between television and morality ultimately turns away from the problem of moral relationships. Of course, for Bauman, that is exactly the issue at hand; the seemingly decisive conquest of the moral by the aesthetic, of responsibility by fun.

What is clear, however, is the point of connection between Bauman and Alain Finkielkraut. They both assume that the suffering other will be overwhelmingly morally compelling to any and every audience only insofar as that other is possessed of a material solidity. When that solidity is absent – as it necessarily must be when the other is present only through representation – moral status is thrown into doubt and there emerges for the audience the pressing problem of what this means. Doubt and uncertainty replace the certainty and confidence which would presumably prevail when and where the other is possessed of a material dimension and integrity. For Finkielkraut the result is that the audience is thrown back into its habitual modes of viewing when it is confronted with uncertainty, while for Bauman the result is that the audience demands to be entertained and amused if the others are going to be able to command anything approaching a second glance or thought (and even then, that ability is dependent upon there being nothing more entertaining on another channel or on the next page).

Yet in subsequent comments, Bauman has put a question mark against the ability of representations and reports of suffering and misery to be entertaining even on their own limited terms. He has done this by emphasizing the problem of global poverty (and therefore the comparison and connection of Bauman with Finkielkraut is given more validity) and by drawing on some comments by the Polish commentator Ryszard Kapuscinski. He points to three areas of concern.

First, Bauman says that it is no coincidence that reports of famines come from those parts of the world which we also tend to associate with the once rapidly growing economies of the 'Asian tigers'. According to Bauman, the audience is left to reach the conclusion that starvation and misery are not inevitable in any part of the world and, therefore, that the suffering must be the fault of the victims in some mysterious yet no doubt decisive manner. The success stories of some Asian economies 'are assumed to demonstrate what was to be proved – that the sorry plight of the hungry and indolent is their *sui generis* choice: alternatives are available, and within reach – but not taken for the lack of industry or resolve'. He concludes that, 'the underlying message is that the poor themselves bear responsibility for their fate' (Bauman 1998a: 73). What this comment seems to miss, however, is the fact that many reports of famine come from Africa. But the general thrust of Bauman's comment remains valid. Africa is invariably presented as a place of endemic and persistent pain and suffering. Therefore, instead of poverty being the fault of the victims, the message is that it is simply the way that things are. It becomes their unalterable fate.

Second, 'the news is so scripted and edited as to reduce the problem of poverty and deprivation to the question of hunger alone' (Bauman 1998a: 73). The point here is that, for Bauman and Kapuscinski alike, the reduction of poverty to hunger represents a gross oversimplification of a complex and multidimensional condition. For them both, poverty is about much more than hunger and starvation and to pretend otherwise is to reduce the issue of global poverty to a straightforward issue which needs to be addressed only when the problem arises. In other words, Western audiences are able to forget about whole swathes of the world so long as they are not seen or known to be experiencing famine. This is because the equation of poverty with hunger means that where there is not hunger neither can there be poverty.

Third, Bauman uses Kapuscinski to suggest that the media coverage of famine, misery and suffering serves to isolate the world of the audience from the world in which it seems that violence and brutality run amok. He says that the media create the world 'out there' as a problem from which the world 'in here' has to be isolated and kept apart. Consequently, 'A synthetic image of the *self-inflicted* brutality sediments in public consciousness – an image of . . . an alien, subhuman world beyond ethics and beyond salvation'. Bauman says that this 'synthetic image' allows audiences to believe that, 'Attempts to save that world from the worst consequences of its own brutality may bring only momentary effects and are bound in the long run to fail'. The reports and representations teach that the world 'out there' is literally and metaphorically hopeless. Indeed, Bauman says that for the audience, the major problem becomes one of how to make sure that the prosecutors of brutality are kept firmly in the 'out there' that is marked by violence and want, in contradistinction to the 'in here' which is purportedly marked by ethics and hope (Bauman 1998: 75–6).

From Finkielkraut and Bauman the conclusion seems to be obvious. There might not be anything which will be able to snap the audience out of its deep and well-learned torpor and boredom, and some of the scenes might be so commonplace that they are scarcely noticed. The implication seems to be that nothing terribly much matters, and nothing matters of its own account, on its own terms.

The intentions of journalists

News producers also know that whatever story they are covering cannot be accorded any status of being absolutely important to the exclusion of everything else (indeed, even if a story is the most important thing that has happened today and even if all news broadcasts are dedicated to it, there is no reason to assume that it will be that significant tomorrow), and they also know that the pressures of time mean that their report will have to draw on a repertoire of stock images and linguistic devices if it is going to be able to make any sense to the audience. The world becomes known through shorthand and the audience know the key to that code only through repetition and more or less enforced learning. Moreover, it is rare for television journalists to be allocated the time they feel that they need in order to adequately report the complexities of any given situation; even when they are given time, the consequences are not necessarily what they intended.

In this respect, a salutary tale has been told by George Alagiah, the former BBC Africa correspondent. He has spoken about two reports he filed from the famine zones of Sudan in 1998. The first report was a fairly conventional piece which told how the famine was hitting the small town of Tonj. It included all of the usual images of hunger and starvation that audiences have come to depend upon if they are going to be able to recognize a famine. Personally I cannot recall either of Alagiah's reports, but I am happy to wager that this first report included pictures of babies suckling at the empty breasts of their mothers, toddlers with flies around their eyes and, quite probably, a picture of two naked children aged about 8 or 9 walking along a dusty track. The report probably included as well pictures of the overwhelmed famine relief facilities. The second report was broadcast the following night. Alagiah thought that the second report was much more challenging than the first of his abilities as a broadcast journalist, and it attempted to contextualize the earlier report of the famine. This second report included interviews with key players from the area, and it is clear that Alagiah is immensely proud of what he filed. Both reports were allocated three minutes of air time.

Now, Alagiah intended the two reports to fit together, with the latter giving the depth and context to the former. But this is not what happened. Certainly, the BBC broadcast the reports as intended, but: 'Ask anyone in our newsroom which piece they remember and they will tell you it is the first, with its harrowing pictures of a famine at work'. Evidently, the wider audience reacted in the same way. Alagiah says that he received a number of letters after the two reports and that, 'Most people remember feeling sorry for the poor souls of southern Sudan but not many can recall being told how the people there had reached that sorry state' (Alagiah 1999: 5).

Alagiah believes that his job has a certain moral significance. He establishes that significance on the need to defend human rights in a world which disregards them all too easily. He says that, 'the reason we need to take action on behalf of the people of Kosovo and Sudan is that, in both cases, human rights are being trampled'. For Alagiah: 'The defence of human rights is a principle. It is an absolute' (Alagiah 1999: 5). Notice how, in those passages, Alagiah draws a causal connection between his ability as a journalist to report and to bring home the realities of the destruction of 'human rights' and action that is taken by audiences on behalf of those who are so suffering. Alagiah wants his audiences to do something on the basis of what he reports, and his problem is that the audiences might well do nothing at all or, alternatively, that they might not do what he intended. Alagiah wants political mobilization and outrage. He wants a commitment on the part of media audiences to alleviate and to deplore the suffering that is brought home to them. But this is not what Alagiah sees around him. What he sees instead is little more than *sympathy*. He says that, 'I am the last person to deride the emotional response that viewers had to some of my reports, but the danger of feeling sorry for someone is that it can be a somewhat ephemeral reaction. It lasts only until some other tragedy eclipses it'. He does not just want people to care. He wants them to care, 'for the right reasons' (Alagiah 1999: 5; the problem of the transience of sympathy and compassion is a theme that I tackle in Tester 1997).

An argument for the moral relevance and importance of the broadcast report has also been made by the former BBC war correspondent, Martin Bell. Writing after the war in the Balkans of the early and mid-1990s, Bell expressed his belief that, 'journalism – not only in the war zones and amid human suffering, but perhaps especially there – is not a neutral and mechanical undertaking but in some sense a moral enterprise'. He said that journalism 'must be informed by an idea of right and wrong. It operates frequently on morally dangerous ground. It makes a difference' (Bell 1998: 18). And Bell could give examples from the Balkans war of the difference that television can make. He says that prisoner exchanges would not have happened without the presence of television as some kind of guarantor of the honour of both sides, and he believes that war crimes are harder to perpetrate when the aggressors know that journalists might uncover what they have done (unfortunately, such a possibility did not unduly slow the deeds of Serbian militia).

What Bell is calling for is a morally serious and engaged form of journalism. He calls this a **journalism of attachment** and distinguishes it from what he calls **bystander's journalism**. Bystander's journalism is the tradition in which Bell was trained at the BBC. In the context of war reporting, this kind of journalism focuses on the events as they unfold and on military tactics rather than upon 'the people who provoke them, the people who fight them and the people who suffer from them'. Meanwhile, the journalism of attachment is 'a journalism that cares as well as knows; that is aware of its responsibilities; that will not stand neutrally between good and evil, right and wrong, the victim and the oppressor'. A powerful expression of Bell's journalism of attachment was provided by the press journalist Ed Vulliamy, who covered the Balkans war for *The Guardian*. He once asked: 'What the hell was so confusing or complicated about concentration camps or kids being blown to bits by mortar bombs? What was the problem about whose "side" to be on: the children or the bombers?' (Vulliamy 1997; see also Vulliamy 1994). According to Bell this kind of journalism is all the more necessary because 'we in the press, and especially in television, which is its most powerful division, do not stand apart from the world. We are part of it. We exercise a certain influence, and we have to know that. The influence may be for better or for worse, and we have to know that too' (Bell 1998: 16; see also Bell 1996a).

Once again, it is worth noting that, just like George Alagiah, Martin Bell believes that there is a connection between the reports he and his colleagues file and the action that ensues on the part of the audience. Bell is sure that journalists exercise 'certain influence' and so he too is assuming that the audience (among other constituencies), acts in terms of the extent to which he is successful in showing the evil and the wrong. But Vulliamy is not so sure. He seems to be extremely aware that all of his efforts did not really cause too much audience action and he wonders about the kind of people we seem to have become: 'We shoved all this stuff into the face of homo-supposedly-sapiens as it was happening in 1992' (Vulliamy 1997). And the horrors of that war still went on, without any mobilization of outrage, indeed with relatively few expressions of outrage (few relative to the enormity of what we all knew was happening – concentration camps, rape centres, torture and the rest).

These journalists are agreed that there is a moral component to what it is that they do. They are all agreed that they are professionally and humanly motivated by what might be called a 'journalistic conscience' in which 'the journalist, insofar as he or she is a human being, must strive to alleviate suffering' (Schroth 1995: 45). Alagiah wants to file reports which respect human rights, and which encourage the audience to do likewise. Martin Bell advocates a journalism which knows when it is important to stop being 'objective' and when, instead, it is important to reveal evil and express repugnance and outrage. Ed Vulliamy advocates a passionate journalism that knows what is wrong and which refuses to allow the audience to maintain that it did not know what was happening. For all three of them, the report is assumed to be morally compelling, and their words are riddled with a sense of anxiety that they might not succeed in getting the point over with enough power and clarity, with guilt that they have failed adequately to reflect what they have seen and with dismay that audiences evidently can bear to know all of this and still do very little about it.

There is then a gulf between the moral intentionality of journalists and the moral action that audiences carry out on the basis of what those journalists have reported. For example, Alagiah wants unflinching and non-negotiable respect for human rights in a way which will cause media audiences to spot abuse wherever it happens and to protest against it. But he is aware that this is not at all what his audiences seem to do. Instead of adopting a rigorous **ethical** stance, his viewers and listeners instead become possessed of a more or less temporary sympathy which will likely dissipate into thin air as soon as the next problem comes along.

Conclusion

The point I am wanting to make is that reports of the suffering of distant others are morally meaningful to audiences in a way that is much more complex and confusing than journalists intend. Their meanings also seem to be much more complex than the existing social theories which deal with the matter seem to be able to accommodate. On the one hand, journalists see their productions spinning out of their control and, on the other hand, audiences can sometimes be much more active and questioning than the general theoretical statements which are made by Finkielkraut and Bauman would lead us to expect.

It is precisely this complexity which any detailed consideration of the relationship between compassion, morality and the media has to be able to contain and explain. The remainder of this book offers the resources for one such explanation.

Further reading

Alagiah, G. (1999) New light on the Dark Continent, *The Guardian* (media section), 3 May: 4–5.

Bell, M. (1996a) *In Harm's Way: Reflections of a War-Zone Thug* (revised edition). Harmondsworth: Penguin.

Bell, M. (1998) The journalism of attachment, in M. Kieran (ed.) *Media Ethics*. London: Routledge.

Vulliamy, E. (1997) Being there, *The Guardian* (review section), 9 May: 2–3 and 22.

2 | COMPASSION FATIGUE AND THE ETHICS OF THE JOURNALISTIC FIELD

Introduction

Compassion fatigue means becoming so used to the spectacle of dreadful events, misery or suffering that we stop noticing them. We are bored when we see one more tortured corpse on the television screen and we are left unmoved as soon as we realize that the earthquake in Taiwan killed fewer people than the earthquake in Turkey. Compassion fatigue means being left exhausted and tired by those reports and ceasing to think that anything at all can be done to help. After all, there is bound to be another earthquake in Turkey sooner or later. If it is bigger than the last one it will just overwhelm us so that there is nothing we can do to help. Yet if the earthquake is smaller than the last one, well, it cannot have been that bad really and, so, there is nothing that needs to be done. Compassion fatigue means a certain fatalism. It leads to the conclusion that this is just the way things are and nothing can be done that will make a difference. Compassion fatigue tells us that giving money to help famine relief in Ethiopia will do nothing to stop the starvation next time and that to empathize with the victims of ethnic cleansing will not stop them becoming the perpetrators of atrocity when they get the opportunity. As an editorial piece in *The Times* once said, we have learnt 'the weary conviction that these are countries beyond hope. That is the meaning of compassion fatigue' ('Putting the victims first', *The Times*, 20 July 1991).

It is the purpose of this chapter of the book to explore compassion fatigue. The chapter is not really concerned to examine whether or not compassion fatigue 'exists'. Rather, this chapter seeks to use the phrase 'compassion fatigue' as a route into a series of debates about the ethics of journalistic practice and, thereby, of finding a way into the terrain that the rest of the book will examine. This chapter is more concerned with some of the sociological stakes of the debate about compassion fatigue than it is concerned with the alleged phenomenon itself. Indeed, the chapter builds on the distinct possibility that a discussion about compassion fatigue can be more interesting than the charge that the concept contains.

An account of journalistic compassion fatigue

Evidently, compassion fatigue is not felt by audiences alone. Many journalists have also argued that they have become inured to the sight of suffering, misery or devastation, and many of them wonder if there is some connection between their own sense of apathy and what they take to be the indifference of their readers and viewers. Are journalists responsible for the sense of fatalism that seems to be so widespread?

One of the most engaged and pertinent explorations of this problem is provided by the journalist Janine di Giovanni, in an article published in 1994. She covered the war in the Balkans and witnessed the famine and bloodshed in Somalia and Rwanda during the early to mid-1990s. Di Giovanni wrote that photographers of the genocide in Rwanda left nothing unshown and invisible, but that many of them felt little or no concern for the people whose corpses and despair they pictured. They had become tired by all the suffering and destruction, as had di Giovanni herself. It had become mind-numbingly inevitable for them. All of the journalists had become the weary observers of a world in which another day brings another new pile of bodies. (In the following discussion, I use the label 'journalists' as a shorthand for photographers and reporters. Of course, these groups have different journalistic practices, but from the point of view of the concerns of this discussion they can be pulled together.)

Still, di Giovanni rejects the idea that the photographers and reporters are simply heartless. Quite correctly, she tries to do something rather more *sociological* by attempting to relate the private worries and sensibilities of journalists to public issues about how much suffering we can bear to see (the claim that di Giovanni's approach is sociological draws on the definition of the sociological imagination in Mills 1959). She sees journalists as the victims of their vocation and speculates that compassion fatigue emerges as a defence mechanism on the part of journalists and thereafter audiences alike. They cannot respond emotionally to so much dreadful news without falling into neurosis and there is a psychological 'switching off' by way of protection from the overwhelmingly terrible world.

But which comes first: the switching off of the journalists or the audiences? According to di Giovanni, the former switch off first. She states that, 'If the media is experiencing cynicism and compassion fatigue, then it certainly must be transmitting it to the readers and the viewers. It is not so much callousness or even insensitivity, but information overload'. She continues to fill in some of the details of that overload: 'In the past four years, we have steadily moved from crisis to crisis, from images of death, destruction, chaos and madness; the Romanian orphans, the siege of Sarajevo, the Somalian civil war' (di Giovanni 1994). In other words, the photographers and reporters – just like their viewers and readers – have been emotionally overwhelmed by all the horror they have witnessed. The only way they can keep on working, viewing or reading is by detaching themselves in such a way that where there might have been engagement and compassion, there is instead weariness and apathy.

For a writer who is as thoughtful as Janine di Giovanni, the phrase 'compassion fatigue' begins to approach the level of a fairly sophisticated sociological category which can be used to analyse and make sense of a whole range of emotional engagements with the press, broadcasting and the world that those media seek to report or represent. Indeed, the way she develops her analysis of compassion fatigue links the term to debates in academic literature about the relationships between analysts or field researchers and their subjects (see for example Carbonell and Figley 1996). But, nevertheless, in the context of debates about press and broadcasting, the phrase takes for granted much more than it manages to explain. Indeed, beneath its surface plausibility, di Giovanni's account of compassion fatigue makes a number of assumptions which are questionable at best and untenable at worst.

First, if di Giovanni is right with her contention that compassion fatigue arises as journalists become more and more tired of seeing suffering and misery, she is required by the logic of her narrative to assume some kind of 'golden age' in the past when 'switching off' was not the dominant response. Her narrative requires her to make such an assumption either about the journalists around her (that is to say, they used to be compassionate as *individuals*, but they are not any more) or she has to make that assumption about the profession of journalism taken as a whole (journalists *as a group* used to be compassionate but they are not anymore). In either case, the narrative assumption is that the engagement of journalists with what they saw was formerly very different indeed than it is today. Here then, di Giovanni's account of compassion fatigue necessary requires the assumption of a personal or historical past in which compassion was not fatigued, and in which journalists did not pass by the new pile of bodies with scarcely a grimace. By the logic of

her narrative then, di Giovanni is telling a story of the decline and fall of journalistic conscience and of the conscience of journalists. Quite simply, the
problem with this narrative is that there might be little or no historical evidence to support it. On the contrary, it is not at all far-fetched to contend that
today journalists are much more compassionate than they ever used to be.
Certainly it is not unreasonable to make that counter-assertion.

Second, when di Giovanni claims that contemporary journalists have
'switched off' because they have become immune to the sight and stench of
suffering, she is implying a general psychological trait of all journalists
everywhere. Or at least, she is implying such a common state for any journalists who have been in the field for any length of time and who have had
the first flush of enthusiasm shaken off. But if that is indeed the case, the
problem which confronts the narrative is one of explaining how it can possibly be that some journalists actually *do* care about some instances of misery
even though they have seen much worse suffering before. How can di Giovanni's thesis about compassion fatigue explain those instances when some
journalists – even perhaps the most experienced and cynical – do feel compassion in a way that they did not before? The justification for the claim that
this is not a speculative criticism is provided by di Giovanni's essay itself.
What she is saying is that by the time she reached places like Somalia and
Sarajevo, her ability to suffer with the suffering of others had been severely
dented if not, in fact, terminally prejudiced. She found that she did not care
any more. But, quite simply, if di Giovanni did not care any more then it is
scarcely likely that she would care that she had ceased to care. The fact that
di Giovanni wrote an essay about her increasing inability to care shows that
she *does* care. The logic of the narrative of compassion fatigue is that the
possibility of a kind of bond between the journalists and the other has been
so stretched that the photographer or the reporter is no longer able to feel it.
But di Giovanni precisely does still feel the pull of the thread. If her compassion were entirely fatigued she would not be worried about the fate of
her ability to feel compassion.

Third, implicit to the narrative of compassion fatigue is a normative
assumption that people are and will be compassionate towards one another.
Yet Michael Ignatieff has contended that although audiences (and it might
be added, journalists) might feel themselves to be moved by pictures of the
suffering of others, there is nothing either necessary or natural about that
feeling. Rather: 'Behind the seemingly natural mechanics of empathy at
work in viewers' response to these images lies a history by which their con-
sciences were formed to respond as they do' (Ignatieff 1998: 12). That history of moral conscience is taken by Ignatieff to be the history of a European
ideal of moral **universalism**. He says that moral universalism is the claim

that social differences do not justify the different treatment of human beings and, moreover, that all humans have the same needs precisely because of their shared and common humanity. Within moral universalism then, it is believed that there are common and definite bonds of mutual responsibility and **solidarity** that tie all people together regardless of their social characteristics and attributes. Moral universalism is identified by Ignatieff as having its roots in the Christian promise of a salvation that ignores the distinction between masters and slaves and he says that this claim about unity and equality feeds into European jurisprudence. It also implies the classical liberal ideal of tolerance. Ignatieff argues that the specific events of the twentieth century have meant that this claim about moral universalism has led to a general situation of what amounts to a 'siding with the victim' (Ignatieff 1998: 25).

The ethic of compassion fatigue

It is clear from the way that she discusses it that, whatever the problems of her approach, Janine di Giovanni understands compassion fatigue to be one of the defining traits of journalistic practice in the present. She is in little doubt that it does exist. To this extent, di Giovanni is seeking to *describe* the moral horizons of photographers and reporters. She is seeking to establish what *is* the case. But there is something else going on in her discussion. More interestingly and importantly, she is concerned and worried that her colleagues and her self have evidently ceased to be able to feel any sympathy towards or connection with those whom they interview and whose corpses they gaze upon. For di Giovanni this is morally and ethically problematic. It is an issue that demands attention.

As such, di Giovanni's comments on compassion fatigue are also shot through with a sense that all of this is wrong and unacceptable. In this way di Giovanni's treatment of the issue also contains a *judgement* of compassion fatigue. She does not just describe. Or at least, her description is shaped by a commitment to what she believes *ought* to be the case in journalistic practice. The treatment of what *is* from the point of view of an *ought* is the basis of an *ethical* argument about journalistic practice and a critique of what presently prevails.

The ethical critique is present within di Giovanni's comments because, although she focuses upon what she takes to be the fact of compassion fatigue, she approaches it from the perspective of a number of implicit assumptions about what the nature of the bond between the journalists and the victims *ought* to be. Janine di Giovanni's essay contains within its narrative a premise about what *ought* to be the case (journalists ought to feel compassion for those whom they photograph or report) which is taken to be contrary to what *is* the case (journalists do not feel such compassion). That premise shapes and is reflected in her conclusions about compassion fatigue. Quite simply, compassion fatigue is a problem and, indeed, intelligible as an issue, only if one starts with the premise that there *ought* to be some bond of sympathy between the journalists and the victims. If one did not start with that premise then there could be no ethical and moral problem of compassion fatigue. For example, if I were a war reporter whose work was guided by the premise that I ought to report what happens 'without fear or favour' and that it is my job to tell viewers and readers what is going on rather than what it feels like to witness all of this, then I will not be worried by notions of compassion fatigue in my professional life. I will not be so worried because compassion is not one of the premises underpinning and informing my work. It is only because di Giovanni takes as given the compassion of journalists that she is able to talk about the fatigue of that emotional link.

One thing that di Giovanni does not draw out is the basis of her statements of the ought. Where does the *ought* come from? What validates it? That part of her essay is missing but, if it is reconstructed, the whole issue of compassion fatigue, which seems to be so self-evident and obvious at a first glance, begins to become more complex. However, even in that complication it becomes more interesting. Perhaps the most basic premise behind di Giovanni's judgement of contemporary journalistic practice concerns compassion itself. She takes the validity and significance of compassion for granted, never questions it nor seeks to enquire as to what it might mean and entail. Yet, if Ignatieff is right, these kinds of moral horizons might not warrant that status of the self-evident.

Compassion can be defined as suffering with the suffering of an other. Natan Sznaider has discussed compassion in slightly more technical terms and he has defined it as, 'an active moral demand to address others' suffering. Directed toward those outside the scope of personal knowledge, it becomes public compassion, shaping moral obligations to strangers in the arenas of civil society and liberal democracy' (Sznaider 1998: 117). In these terms, it becomes possible to clarify the constituency and the horizons of the kind of compassion that is said to have been exhausted by the emergence of compassion fatigue. The problem is not the relationships of the photographer or the reporter to their immediate family or neighbours. No claim is being made of the order that the journalist who walks away from a pile of corpses with a shrug of the shoulders is a callous and heartless sadist who cares about nothing. Rather, and this is what the passage from Sznaider does make it possible to see, compassion involves the addressing of the suffering *of others* in the *public* sphere. The nub of the issue of compassion fatigue, then, is not the nastiness of the journalist but, instead, the nature of the moral demand that is made by those who are strangers and the nature of the moral engagement that the individual feels towards those whom she or he does not know or with whom she or he has any prior relationships. Compassion fatigue is about *public* compassion.

Sznaider makes the valid claim that public compassion 'must be distinguished from earlier models of compassion like religious charity, as well as later models like the bureaucratic welfare state' (Sznaider 1998: 119). Although Sznaider himself does not develop this claim, it can be suggested that public compassion is different from religious charity because such charity did not necessarily require a constituency of the public (where the public is defined as a community of strangers). Within Christian narratives for example, the horizon of the public was occluded by commitment to others either as the community of humanity made in the image of God, as the community of believers or as the concern to secure individual salvation. For example, and by way of an illustration of the first of these possibilities (and indeed by way of a confirmation of Ignatieff's point about Christian moral universalism), Saint Augustine wrote that 'all people must be reckoned as neighbours . . . [T]he person to whom compassion must be shown and the person by whom it must be shown to us are rightly called neighbours' (Augustine 1997: 23). Meanwhile, the welfare state – some might argue – replaces moral obligations towards strangers with the concerns of the rights and responsibilities of citizenship (Marshall 1977).

According to Sznaider, contemporary public compassion has its most important roots in the emergence of market economies and contractual social relationships since the spread of the market expands the sphere of strangers about whom the individual needs to care and with whom the individual is required to relate in some way (Sznaider 1998: 121). However, the rise of an ethic of compassion also has roots in ideas and sensibilities about the constraints of the world. Indeed, it could be suggested that ideas and sensibilities are more important in the formation of public compassion than contracts or markets. After all, market demands can easily imply the treatment of others as means to an end, and that possible treatment allows no necessary space for emotional bonds.

Hannah Arendt's book *On Revolution* (Arendt 1973a) points out that, historically, the spectacle of suffering and misery has not always moved the viewer to feel compassion. That emotional bond is socially and historically specific. For example, Arendt discusses European visitors to America during the years around the American and French Revolutions. Some of these Europeans would have been prepared to argue that the suffering of the other justifies a revolution in France but they never made a similar argument about America when they saw the suffering of the slaves. The point that Arendt is wanting to make is that initially it was only in the European context that suffering and misery became associated with ideals of compassion whereas, in the context of America, the suffering of the slaves was taken to be simply the way that things are, the way that things were meant to be (Arendt 1973a: 71). Or, to put it another way, if Arendt is right, the founders of the American republic could never have felt anything that we might now call compassion fatigue for the simple reason that they were not compassionate in the first place. What this means is that compassion is not a natural, innate or inevitable ethic. As Arendt says: 'History tells us that it is by no means a matter of course for the spectacle of misery to move men to pity'. It has seemed to be natural and innate only since the eighteenth century: 'Since then, the passion of compassion has haunted and driven the best men of all revolutions' (Arendt 1973a: 70, 71).

The question which needs to be answered is, then, what happened in the eighteenth century to make 'the best men' become possessed of the ethic of compassion? Sznaider offers a variety of answers. Perhaps despite claims elsewhere in his analysis of compassion, the discussion leads to the conclusion that the possession of the ethic was not *only* due to the development and spread of trade and contractual relationships between strangers. He also implies that it was due to the spread of humanitarian ideals and to the emergence of a romantic sensibility of the 'man of feeling' (Sznaider 1998). In these terms it could be argued that the European visitors to America failed to be moved by the spectacle of the suffering of the slaves simply because there was no contractual relationship linking them together and, more disturbingly, simply because the visitors did not identify the slaves as morally relevant (that is to say, the slaves were not recognized as humans whose suffering was of actual or potential moral consequence). The slaves did not move the Europeans as men (and presumably sometimes as women) of feeling.

Arendt offers a different account of what happened in the eighteenth century. She says that compassion emerged as and when it became impossible to 'avert one's eyes from the misery and unhappiness of the mass of humankind'. She suggests that, 'the point of the matter is that only the predicament of poverty, and not either individual frustration nor social ambitions, can arouse compassion' (Arendt 1973a: 73). Poverty became inescapable not simply in a visual sense (the poor and destitute were all around) but, for Arendt much more importantly, in a political sense as soon as the poor became the subjects of political movements which proposed that poverty and suffering ought to be pitied and that they can be remedied. Compassion is consequently linked to a belief that the world does not have to be like this. It implies that the existing organization of the world is wrong and that it ought to be and can be changed. Once again then it is possible to see the ethical dimension. According to Arendt, compassion involves a judgement of what *is* the case (the inescapable fact of poverty) from the point of view of a commitment to what *ought* to be the case (poverty ought to be remedied and resolved; it is a problem to be overcome). Politics thus becomes the programme of resolving the problem of poverty. However, it can be suggested that the horizon of compassion has broadened far beyond an exclusive emphasis upon poverty alone. This is because the focus on poverty provided a point of entry into a wider concern with, and problematization of, the fundamental needs and well-being of others. It opens up the whole agenda of what humans need to live and, by a reverse, it makes it possible to recognize an affront to common humanity when these needs are not met thanks to either circumstance, relationships or violence. In this way, poverty has tended to become one dimension of a wider judgement and critique of suffering and misery.

Now, it is exactly this gap which Arendt identifies, between the visibility and recognition of the presence of suffering and the contention that it requires remedy, that is the historical basis of the ethical judgement which journalists like Janine di Giovanni wish to be able to make when they gaze upon the spectacles of piles of corpses. The key difference between the eighteenth century visitor to America and the contemporary journalist is that the recognition of suffering has been expanded and the ethic of compassion has been universalized (this claim is intended to recall the comments by Ignatieff which were cited earlier in this chapter). Poverty, misery and suffering have become identified as offences to humanity as such rather than to just certain sections of it (so that, were slave labour to be found today, the misery of the prisoners would be the first thing to be noticed rather than the last). In this way compassion has been universalized.

Following Ignatieff, universalization can be explained as a product and a consequence of the logic of legal codes which take *humanity* as their referent and subject, rather than just the citizens of one particular nation state. Undoubtedly, this universalization indicates the connection of compassion with the paternalism of nineteenth century European projects of 'civilization' in which the others were to be encouraged to become more like 'us' and they do require critical scrutiny. For example, some critics, following from Nietzsche and into deconstructionism and the suspicion towards metanarratives, would point to the way in which claims about universal human qualities, capacities or dimensions are all made by particular social and cultural groups. They would cast doubt on Ignatieff's story, and upon all talk about common properties and qualities or about some unitary 'civilization', by examining exactly who it is who says this (and by that token it would not be coincidental that Ignatieff is a white male). Yet it remains valid to contend that even though such projects are violent and oppressive towards the others, patronize and belittle the others, they do nevertheless presume some common identity between 'them' and 'us' even if that identity is turned towards the utilitarianism of what 'they' can do for 'us' (quite simply, without such a presumption of identity, projects of 'civilization' would have been impossible to conceptualize and conceive. Here I have been using the word 'civilization' in its everyday sense rather than as a technical sociological category after Norbert Elias).

However, a further question emerges. If it is relatively easy to uncover the historical contingency (that is, the lack of historical necessity and inevitability) and inflections of the ethic of compassion, why do journalists such as di Giovanni worry when their sense of compassion is 'fatigued'? If compassion is not necessary why is it felt to be so terrible when it is absent? The most simple answer to that question is that journalists worry about compassion fatigue because, insofar as they are the heirs to a history of ethical subjectivity into which they (like us) have been socialized, the absence of a feeling for a common bond between all humanity is tantamount to a repudiation of the humanity of she or he who so fails to feel. In other words, journalists worry about compassion fatigue because they might feel that they have ceased to be human in some fundamental manner. They might also be worried about the possibility that a lack of compassion might be taken by peers to be a sign of an absence of one of the integral parts of being human. Perhaps this explains the air of desperation that pervades so much of di Giovanni's essay. She is concerned about her own human being and her own ethical integrity. Perhaps this also explains why she cares so much about her evident inability to care for others anymore. She sees that inability, that failure to feel, as an undermining of her own humanity in the regard of herself and her peers.

All of this is undoubtedly valid, but there is another way of approaching an answer to this question. Instead of focusing on the ethical subjectivity of the individual journalist, this alternative answer stresses the ethics of *journalistic practice*. Consequently, it avoids the trap of personalizing and individualizing compassion fatigue in such a way that it is concluded that journalists are simply uncaring. This alternative seeks to relate journalistic practice to the sociological relationships and structures of the field of journalistic production.

Compassion in the field of practice

With the phrase 'field of journalistic practice', a gesture is being made towards the work of the French sociologist, Pierre Bourdieu. Bourdieu writes that a field may be understood as 'a structured social space, a field of forces, a force field. It contains people who dominate and others who are dominated. Constant, permanent relationships of inequality operate inside this space, which at the same time becomes a space in which the various actors struggle for the transformation or preservation of the field' (Bourdieu 1998: 40). Bourdieu is wanting to make it plain that journalistic practice is not reducible to the choices and idiosyncrasies of individual photographers and journalists. Rather, practice is shaped in fundamental if not indeed determining ways by the structures of the journalistic field. Like all fields (Bourdieu 1984), this one is structured around relationships of inequality and struggles of dominance and subordination. Journalistic production will be shaped and determined by the position which the individual photographer or reporter occupies in the field; do they work for a national broadcaster (such as the BBC) or for a commercial network? Are they a freelance or a staff member? Are they an expert in this particular story or just a 'talking head' flown in a few hours before, flown out a few minutes after filing the report? The answers to those kinds of questions have an impact upon what the journalist is likely to say or do and upon the representation or the report that is produced. As Bourdieu puts it in a methodological comment: 'if I want to find out what one or another journalist is going to say or write, or will find obvious or unthinkable, normal or worthless, I have to know the position that journalist occupies in this space [i.e. the journalistic field]' (Bourdieu 1998: 41).

According to Bourdieu the journalistic field emerged as a sociologically identifiable entity during the nineteenth century. Yet that emergence was itself organized in terms of, and riddled by, a conflict between two different interpretations of the role and rationale for journalistic practice. Bourdieu identifies a conflict between 'newspapers offering "news," preferably "sensational" or better yet, capable of creating a sensation, and newspapers featuring analysis and "commentary," which marked their difference from the other group by loudly proclaiming the values of "**objectivity**"' (Bourdieu 1998: 70; see note 1). Within this field, each of the two oppositional groups had its own criteria of what *ought* to be done and therefore each was – and remains – identified with its own particular ethic and mode of judgement of the world.

For the camp which vested its dominance upon its purported objectivity, journalistic practice is legitimate (right and appropriate) to the extent that it is recognized as being authoritative – or at least credible – by peers. It follows that the most legitimate – the most dominant – photographer or reporter will be those who are identified by their peers as the consistent producer of authoritative commentary. Perhaps this explains why war photographers such as Don McCullin or Kevin Carter are so frequently discussed and applauded by their fellow journalists and elevated to something like a pedestal of excellence, even though the wider public (who have certainly seen their pictures and read or watched the productions of similar reporters) are probably unaware of their names. From this point of view, market forces and imperatives are of ostensibly lesser concern than the 'pure' values of objectivity and fact-based commentary. Meanwhile, the camp which is organized around the values of **sensationalism** is accorded a certain legitimacy to the extent that it manages to secure, 'recognition by the public at large, which is measured by numbers of readers, listeners, or viewers, and therefore, in the final analysis, by sales and profits' (Bourdieu 1998: 70). Bourdieu is confident that in this conflict, that side which is most easily and readily able to accommodate the demands of the market will ultimately be able to secure the greatest influence. It will be more able to get the exclusive news stories and, moreover, it will operate more quickly and flexibly. Those who accommodate the market are more able and willing to produce the perishable commodities that news, just like markets themselves, demand and require (Bourdieu 1998: 71).

These might seem to be fairly abstract points but the validity of Bourdieu's analysis is borne out if attention is briefly paid to some of the debates which developed in the wake of Martin Bell's call for a journalism of attachment. For a number of commentators, such a journalism would have meant nothing other than an undermining of the standards of objectivity and impartiality upon which the BBC (for whom Bell was a correspondent) had been founded. Moreover, the debate highlights the ambivalent position of the ethic of compassion in the journalistic field. Bell has already been mentioned in this book but, to recall, quickly, after he returned from the war in the Balkans of the early to mid-1990s, he started to reflect critically upon his journalistic practice. Bell said that he had been 'brought up in the old and honourable tradition of balanced, dispassionate, objective journalism . . . I would move from war zone to war zone without being greatly affected by any of them'. The implication of this passage is that Bell would not have worried about compassion fatigue because his journalistic practice was neither shaped nor influenced by a suffering with others. But the Balkans war made Bell believe that this approach was no longer tenable: 'what I believe in now is what I prefer to call the journalism of attachment; a journalism that knows as well as cares' (Bell 1996b). This advocacy did not meet with universal approval. For example, Lucian Hudson, a senior editor of the BBC's 24 hour news service, was moved to personal insult in reply to Bell's claim that rolling news militates against any kind of attachment because it is too fast and shallow. Hudson said that Bell 'sounds like a celibate priest who at a certain stage in his life has decided to go and bonk. The temptation to get engaged is just too great and he wants to get stuck in'. A more sober, considered and less gratuitously nasty critique of Bell was offered by Andrew Marr, then editor of *The Independent* newspaper. He offered the view that the journalism of attachment has a place on opinion and editorial pages but that, 'viewers and readers still want cold facts and need the time and space to make considered judgements' (the comments by Hudson and Marr are taken from Culf 1996).

What is interesting about the debate which this argument inspired is the way it highlights the ambiguous ethical position of the journalist. The journalist – and journalistic production – is torn between objectivity and human attachment. And this example can be used to highlight gaps in Bourdieu's account of the journalistic field. Undoubtedly, Bourdieu is quite right to stress the opposition between the positions of what might be termed 'pure' and sensationalist 'market' journalism, but the logic of his sociology is to reduce all questions of ethics and morality to the struggle for legitimacy and distinction within those respective positions (Sayer 1999). Bourdieu does not adequately appreciate the possibility – indeed the distinct likelihood – that within the journalistic field there is also a central ambiguity about the ethical relevance and content of journalistic practice and production. That ambiguity is a product of the fact that the journalist is her or himself the subject of two different ethical logics. This was hinted at in a comment by Eason Jordan, vice-president of CNN International, in response to Bell's argument. Jordan said: 'If you are a real human being you have compassion and feelings. As long as you are accurate and fair, to be compassionate is acceptable for a reporter' (from Culf 1996).

At first glance, Jordan's attempt to bring Bell's journalism of attachment together with objective reporting seems to be eminently sensible and distinctly viable. But a closer inspection reveals that the two logics – towards compassion and impartiality – do not necessarily go together. This is exactly the dilemma which Martin Bell was trying to think through. The concern to be 'accurate and fair' is legitimized by the side of the field of journalistic practice which associates news with objectivity and, at most, a commentary which is clearly based in the 'facts' of the case. This concern can easily require journalists to put into abeyance their emotional engagement with what they have witnessed. To be accurate and fair means *not* to be influenced by immediate reactions. For Bell, of course, a journalistic practice which upholds these values, and which claims legitimacy and authority precisely by reference to standards of impartiality, represents nothing more than an abdication of the common humanity between the journalists and the victims. Yet the concern to be a 'real human being' militates against objectivity and impartiality. This second concern owes more to the demands of the market and to sensationalism in the field of journalistic production and it elevates one particular meaning of humanity (the meaning of the universalized emotional bond of compassion and a certain empathy) to the place of primary importance. In these terms, the 'facts' can easily become less significant than the demonstrable humanity of the journalist and, moreover, objectivity can come to seem like callous indifference.

But if Bourdieu's speculations are correct, this struggle between two different positions within the journalistic field is beginning to reach some kind of conclusion. According to him, the increased competition between television institutions has entailed, 'the increased influence of the most cynical and most successful seekers after anything sensational' (Bourdieu 1998: 50) and, consequently, news broadcasts (as products of the field of journalistic practice and production) have tended to become ever more like tabloid newspapers in order to secure market share: 'Pushed by competition for marketshare, television networks have greater and greater recourse to the tried and true formulas of tabloid journalism, with emphasis . . . devoted to human interest stories or sports'. Bourdieu goes on: 'In short, the focus is on those things which are apt to arouse curiosity but require no analysis, especially in the political sphere' (Bourdieu 1998: 51). The implication of Bourdieu's speculation is that ostensibly objective and impartial journalism is of decreasing significance because it is incompatible with the demand for market share. Meanwhile, bringing this point together with Martin Bell's advocacy of committed journalism, a journalism of attachment is likely to become all the more appealing than his 'bystander's journalism' (indeed, a reflection of this tendency is the pejorative tone of the very phrase 'bystander's journalism'). But it is unlikely to be the kind of journalism that Bell himself would wish to promote. It is likely to be much more trite than anything Bell would advocate since, whatever else he might desire, Bell never gives up on the need for objectivity. His point is that certain facts require and demand a certain ethical response. He is not saying that the immediate response should wholly dominate objective reporting. But the logic of Bourdieu's argument is that this is quite possibly the direction in which journalism might be headed. Traces of it can be seen in the frequency with which journalists refer to 'I': 'I saw . . .', 'I felt . . .' and so forth. This represents a replacement of the objective concerns of the journalistic field with the logic of the more sensational human interest. At the very least, it represents a reduction of complex phenomena and events to the immediate responses and feelings of a few individuals (a tendency that is explored in a different context in Tester 1999a; for an example of this tendency, see Keane 1996).

To this extent, even though compassion fatigue is felt by individual photographers and reporters, it does not need to be reduced to their own subjective responses to suffering and misery. Much more importantly compassion fatigue can be identified and interpreted as one reflection of the conflicts and relationships of power and opposition within the field of journalistic production. It is a product of the conflict between two different definitions of what journalistic practice ought to be. And, more broadly, it is a consequence of the contradiction which arises when individuals who are the heirs of a tradition of an ethical subjectivity of compassion and who are trained to be the producers of objective journalism begin to experience the demands and the logic of the market. Compassion fatigue emerges as an issue when objective journalistic practice is challenged by the demands of the sensational and reduced to the 'quick fix' of human interest.

The virtues of journalistic practice

It is perhaps worthwhile pulling together the threads of the preceding points and systematizing them into a set of coherent claims. The argument has been that the travails and tribulations of individual photographers or journalists should not be read as statements of individual, psychological and personal failures or anxieties. Rather, they should be read *sociologically*. The concerns that these journalists express should be interpreted as results of the tensions which run through the constitution and the determinations of the field of journalistic practice. In these terms, compassion fatigue can be interpreted as one manifestation of the tension between the values of 'pure' and market led journalistic practice. To this extent, the claims of this discussion are wholly compatible with points that are raised by Pierre Bourdieu.

However, Bourdieu's analysis of the field of journalistic practice pays little or no heed to the ethical subjectivity of the photographers and reporters. And that is precisely what does need to be emphasized. Their ethical subjectivity has three dimensions. First, it is moulded by the history of the ethic of compassion of which they are the subjects. Second, it is shaped by the kinds of ethical demands which Martin Bell talks about when he critiques that 'bystander's journalism' which, he says, involves reporting the facts objectively without empathizing with the human victims who suffer the consequences of all of the violence and misery. Third, it is shaped by the logic of the market which tends towards a journalistic practice that is sensationalist and oriented around human interest. In sum, it can be said that journalistic practice is therefore possessed of definite and determinate virtues. The difficulty for journalists is that these three sites of **virtue** do not necessarily fit together. Indeed, they tend to divide journalistic practice against itself.

The concept of virtue is embedded within the Aristotelian tradition of ethics (Aristotle 1980). Virtue consists in an habitual disposition on the part of the individual to act in a certain way. Ross Poole (1991) offers the usual example of virtue when he says that, 'thus the virtue of courage (or of charity) is the disposition to act courageously (or charitably) when the occasion arises'. According to this tradition, virtue is not something which is innate within the individual. Instead the acquisition of the disposition to act in a certain way is understood to be the result of education and practice (Poole 1991: 56). In the case of the virtues of journalistic practice, this would mean that the photographer or journalist learns to be objective or sensational through training. The traits of the productions do not, therefore, reflect and represent purely personal quirks. Through that education and practice, the individual comes to possess a moral character so that he or she will always tend to act in a certain manner given the appropriate occasion. Consequently, in this tradition: 'to be moral is to be a certain kind of person and to know how one should act given that one is that kind of person. Morality is a kind of character' (Poole 1991: 56).

This account of virtue has been placed at the heart of the analysis of the present by the moral philosopher Alasdair MacIntyre. He has tied morality (the 'doing' of ethics) to a conception of practice, a word which he uses in a specific and rather technical way. It is worthwhile breaking his definition into a number of parts and discussing each in turn. For MacIntyre, 'practice' consists in, 'any coherent and complex form of socially established cooperative human activity through which goods internal to that form of activity are realized' (MacIntyre 1985: 187). What this means is that MacIntyre does not see practice as something that individuals perform on their own according to entirely idiosyncratic values and criteria. Rather, practice is about social activity that is carried out with others. To this extent, the journalistic field which Bourdieu uncovers can be understood as a field of practice in the sense of MacIntyre insofar as it requires any and every individual to work with and alongside others (for example, the reporter works with the photographer and they both work with the news editor). But, as the quotation establishes, MacIntyre links this practice to the realization of 'goods internal to that form of activity'. Here, MacIntyre is making the point that practice is oriented towards the achievement of some end or other. It is done for a reason.

This claim compares with Bourdieu when he identifies the camps of objective and sensational journalistic practice. MacIntyre would probably read

Bourdieu as saying that these two camps establish standards and ideals of what is 'good' about journalistic practice and, moreover, of what constitutes 'good' for the journalist. From the point of view of a commitment to objective practice, the good is that which impartially and with authority commentates upon the world whereas from the perspective of sensationalist practice, the good is that which bolsters market share and profitability through keeping up to date, human interest and accessibility. The point which needs to be noted is that these goods are not objective standards which are external to these practices but that they are, rather, entirely internal to the practice. In other words, objective journalists cannot stand condemned because they rarely secure high audience ratings. They can be condemned only insofar as their reports are lacking in objectivity. Similarly, the journalistic practice which is shaped by sensationalist values cannot be condemned for lacking in objectivity. It can really be condemned only if it fails to get market share or fails to sustain the interest and engagement of the audience (that engagement can involve the audience buying the newspaper or the broadcaster being able to deliver an audience to advertisers). Similarly, when Martin Bell, by his own admission, was going unmoved from one war zone to another he could not be criticized for being a dispassionate observer because his journalistic practice sought to realize the internal good of objectivity. The realization of that particular internal good is more or less predicated on dispassionate observation. In sum then, and as Alasdair MacIntyre says, the good is internal to the practice and the construction by the individual of a character which is oriented towards the realization of that good (that is internal to the practice but wholly external to the individual her or him self) is the basis of virtue.

Through the practice of virtue, the individual becomes what MacIntyre calls a *character*. At the most obvious level, the word 'character' refers to the distinctive and typical traits of a person. When he uses the word 'character', MacIntyre means that and something more besides. Certainly, MacIntyre equates character with a habitual disposition to act in a typical way (he takes that identification from Aristotle), but he also talks about a wider social and cultural repertoire of characters. MacIntyre says that characters 'are a very special type of social role which places a certain kind of moral constraint on the personality of those who inhabit them' (MacIntyre 1985: 27). Indeed, 'A *character* is an object of regard by the members of the culture generally or by some significant segment of them. He furnishes them with a cultural and moral ideal' (MacIntyre 1985: 29). For MacIntyre then, we come to be and to become characters to the extent that we play a certain social role and accept the moral demands and constraints which that role places upon us. Character is not something that one has; it is something that one *becomes*, in exactly the same way that no actor is Hamlet but he (or possibly she) has to learn to become Hamlet. And, moreover, the standards of whether or not this particular actor is a good Hamlet are entirely internal to the practice of the role of Hamlet although they are external to any given actor (if they were not, there would be no recognizable character called Hamlet).

The situation is comparable with the field of journalistic production. That field establishes certain goods which are internal to journalistic practice. In that practice, individuals play the social role of the journalist and accept the moral constraints which are thereby placed upon them. To the extent that individuals play the role adequately (and the standard of adequacy is established by the extent to which their practice approximates to the internal goods), their individual personality will be fused with the social role and the individual will thus become the personification of a certain moral character for the wider social and cultural context. More or less precisely this kind of process happened to Martin Bell. He was able to practise the character of the committed journalist during the Balkans war and that practice accorded successfully with the internal goods of objectivity and impartiality (despite Bell's own, subsequent, doubts about such 'bystander's journalism'). In that way, his individual personality became fused with the social role to such an extent that he became identified as a man of virtue (and this identification played no small part in Bell's public persona as a morally righteous white-suited independent candidate during the 1997 general election campaign).

Now, it is reasonable to interpret the field of journalistic practice as a context in which journalists become characters in MacIntyre's sense of that word. The field is the terrain of the practice of photographers and reporters and, insofar as their professional character is determined by it, they will become possessed of an habitual disposition to act in one way as opposed to any other. For example, the photographer will become disposed towards making the images which represent what has happened without worrying about the question of whether or not it might have been more appropriate to have intervened rather than have just pressed the shutter. The field establishes the virtues of objectivity and human sensation and therefore establishes for the journalist the virtues of, in Bell's terms, bystander's journalism and the journalism of attachment. But whereas, in the conventional Aristotelian statement, the virtues are non-contradictory (according to Aristotle there is only contradiction because of misunderstanding), within the concrete example of the field of journalistic practice, these two virtues – which simultaneously establish dispositions for the practice of the journalist – are in opposition and, more importantly, present at one and the same time. Hence the characters that are formed within the field of journalistic practice, and which are professionally trained to uphold the peculiar virtues of that field, are riddled by contradiction, doubt and anxiety. On the one hand they have a disposition to inform the public and, on the other hand, they have a disposition to engage as human beings.

For example, Dan Rather, the anchor of the CBS News in the United States, has offered an impassioned discussion of his experiences covering American military involvement in Somalia in 1992. He said that, 'It is an inevitable fact of American journalism, print or electronic, that it shall pro-vide information upon which American citizens will make decisions that affect the outcome of American history. The founders of this nation depended on that fact'. Indeed, 'the media has the responsibility to inform' (Rather 1995: 37). Yet Rather also claims that the 'responsibility to inform' does not only and exclusively involve a statement of the objective facts. He told a story about meeting an 8-year-old girl in one of the refugee camps of Somalia. Harita Muhammed once had five siblings; now she had only one and she was herself a matter of days away from death by starvation. Rather says that he does not know if Harita did die and he has no way of finding out, yet 'I cannot forget her. And I do not think that the American people can forget her, either, or the other children like her.' Rather goes on to ask rhetorical questions which indicate that his journalistic practice is not simply concerned to inform the American public about the objective facts but that it is also shaped by a deep and profound dimension of human inter-est. Dan Rather asks: 'Am I less because I met her? Are the viewers and lis-teners of CBS News less because they know that the Somali people have faces and names? We know that it is not just a matter of tens of thousand of starving people; it is a matter of individuals' (Rather 1995: 36).

In terms of the virtues which are established within the field of journalis-tic practice, Rather can answer all of those questions in the negative. He can be sure that he is not a lesser man because he met Harita, even though he does not know her fate. Instead, he was able to practise and enhance his dis-position for human empathy with the suffering of an other. Similarly, Dan Rather can be sure that the American public was able to demonstrate the virtues of charitableness and concern for the other insofar as his journalistic practice informed them of what was happening in Somalia and thus enabled them to practise pre-existing dispositions: 'the American people do not need television to tell them what is right. The American people do not need tele-vision to tell them what to feel'. This is because: 'The American people make those decisions on their own – based, it is true, on a number of different sources of information, of which television is one, bearing witness as an honest broker of information' (Rather 1995: 36).

The problem is one of how the American people (or any other audience for that matter) can rely upon some such 'honest broker of information' when that information has, itself, been modified by the subjective and emotional responses of the journalist to what she or he has seen. This difficulty can be overcome only if it is contended that, thanks to the determinations of the field of journalistic practice and, in particular, thanks to the kind of virtuous character that it offers, the journalist becomes the representative and the personification of the wider audience. But if that is the case, the journalist has to deal with the empirical problem of how to explain the fact that the audience might not react in the way that the journalist intended or believes to be appropriate in this given situation. This is another of the stakes of the debate about compassion fatigue as it is outlined by Janine di Giovanni. If journalists identify themselves as a representative they must assume that the audience is possessed of much the same moral sensibility as themselves. Consequently, if the journalist is moved by meeting a starving girl, the audience ought also to be so moved. Yet if the audience is not so moved, it has to be concluded that the failure to inspire the virtuous action of compassion does not reside with the audience itself but, rather, with the journalist who must have failed to get the message across sufficiently strongly. This constitutes an extra pressure for the personalization of information (and for the increasing visibility of the journalist, who thus has to begin to tell the audience how to feel). Moreover, it plants the seeds of doubt about the continued compassion of the journalist.

A series of parallel concerns has been explored by Louis D. Boccardi, president and chief executive officer of Associated Press (one of the major news agencies: Allan 1999). He has tried to clarify exactly what is and is not the sphere of responsibility of the journalist when confronted with the suffering of others. He focuses on the question of the relationship between media coverage of an event like the war and famine in Somalia and the foreign policy of nation states. Boccardi develops an ethical argument to advocate that whatever happens in pragmatic terms, the media *ought not* to seek to have any influence over foreign policy. For Boccardi, reporters are engaged in a different enterprise. He believes that they are engaged in *writing* history, not *making* it. This is the context in which Boccardi says that, 'we cover it because it's happening, because our news judgment says this is something the world needs to know about. And that is our function, whether the issue is at the top of any government's agenda, or in the middle, or at the bottom. Or off it'. He declares that it is necessary to let the reporters report and to leave the governors to govern (Boccardi 1995: 47). Boccardi believes that such an ordinance limiting the sphere of influence of journalism is important given the ever increasing speed and volume of the news coverage of relatively distant events. Consequently, for the journalist: 'It is our job to go, sometimes in danger, . . . where there is news. And to try to cover it as fairly and compellingly as we can' (Boccardi 1995: 49). Once again the problem of the contradictory positions in the field of journalistic production can be seen to be undermining the argument. Boccardi does not emphasize the possibility that the concern to cover an event fairly and compellingly can pull the journalist in two different directions.

Both Rather and Boccardi manage to keep at bay some of the oppositions in the field of journalistic production. Not all commentators have been able to reflect with such equanimity. Sometimes the anxieties come to the fore. This seems especially to be the case for those reporters who are always aware that their story is going to have to compete for space with other, equally significant, reports. One such journalist is William Dowell, an American reporter and later editor of considerable experience. Writing from an American perspective, Dowell appears to believe that the Vietnam war represented a key point in the confusion of the motives of the journalist. He compares coverage of Vietnam to reports which were written during the Second World War, and says that the latter often seem to be naïve and almost propagandistic when they are encountered today. He says that they come across as naïve because at the time it was felt that, 'the cause was just, that the struggle was worth the effort, and that the enemy, regardless of his humanity, must be defeated, and that everyone needed to stand together' (Dowell 1995: 69). Now we lack that kind of absolute conviction and confidence. The validity of the Vietnam war was much less clear than that of the Second World War and, in any case, even when it was raging, it was not the bloodiest conflict in the world.

Dowell notes that the war of secession in Bangladesh led to more casualties and refugees than Vietnam. But of this the world was scarcely aware. The problem was that very few American photographers and journalists were in Bangladesh and so that conflict barely registered in the public consciousness. And the journalists who were there knew that the chances of getting their story printed or broadcast were minimal. Dowell claims that: 'There was a cynical rating system among foreign correspondents trying to sell stories to their editors that one American was worth 15 Frenchmen, which were worth 20,000 Africans, which might be worth a million Asians' (Dowell 1995: 69). The only way in which this calculus of death could be bypassed was if the report was able to contain ever-increasing violence in order to secure attention, and 'When a news organization or a reporter begins to rely on the shock effect of war the power inherent in the situation gradually wears off leaving a sour aftertaste' (Dowell 1995: 70–1). Or, it might be said, all that can result is compassion fatigue. It also means that the repertoire of images and of turns of phrase is quickly exhausted so that in the event of subsequent wars, there is nothing new left to say or show. All that can remain is apathy and boredom.

William Dowell's journalistic practice has obviously been marked by a very keen and probably extremely realistic awareness of the demands of the market. To this extent it would seem that his activity has been shaped by the logic of the market alone. But Dowell's comments repay attention because they are not one-dimensional in that way. What is interesting is the way that Dowell's recognition of the demands of the logic of the market causes him to lapse into a certain anxiety about the prospects and possibilities of more objective journalistic practice and motivation. There is indeed a hint of desperation when Dowell tries to build up a case justifying reporting wars in places like Bangladesh even though the reports are unlikely to be printed or broadcast, and despite the fact that few people in the West are likely to care terribly much about what has been happening in that part of Southern Asia (recall Dowell's cynical formula about one American being worth a million Asians). As Dowell asks, 'Why cover wars that no one cares about? . . . On a personal level the only motive that ever really stands the test of time is the desire to know for oneself what is happening and to write history . . . what matters is that history happened, and for whatever reason, someone was there to record it' (Dowell 1995: 74). Yet it does not follow that because someone was there to record history happening, anyone will know or care that history was happening. As such, all Dowell can do when he tries to justify his own journalistic practice is turn away from the sphere of public compassion and, instead, turn inwards towards a personal satisfaction that the virtues of the field of journalistic production have been upheld. But since journalism is, almost by definition and certainly by convention, a practice which consists in public communication it is impossible that a sense of *personal* virtue and that a sense that '*I* was there even though no one hears me' can ever be adequate or satisfying. The anxiety slightly below the surface of Dowell's comments seems to devolve to precisely this realization.

The question of manipulation

It has been one of the key claims of this discussion of the virtues which are established and made possible within the field of journalistic practice that photographers and reporters are likely to be bedevilled by a sense of anxiety and concern for the simple reason that the field of practice is not a monolith. Instead it is characterized by two different logics. These are the logics of objective reporting and of the market. Additionally journalists are the subjects of a broader history of moral sensibility which has emphasized a universalized ethic of compassion.

Commentators like Boccardi attempt to pull together the logics of the field of practice in a series of claims about journalistic virtue which tend to assume that if the full implications of one logic are ameliorated by the implications of the other, then it will be possible for journalistic practice to occupy a median position and thus attend to the concerns of objective reporting and human interest at one and the same time. (This position interestingly compares with the Aristotelian thesis of virtue consisting in the practice of a medial point in any scale of virtue; the crucial difference is of course that in the case of the journalistic field the virtues are incompatible). Yet William Dowell makes it possible to glimpse the personal and subjective costs that such an attempt to occupy the middle ground between two different positions can imply for the individual. Although Dowell is committed to the argument that journalistic practice is worthwhile insofar as it reports on the making of history, he is able to possess any confidence in that claim only if he brushes aside the problem that if history is not being made by the 'right' people in the 'right' places in front of the 'right' reporters, then such events will have little or no news value. This in turn raises an interesting epistemological question as to whether it is actually legitimate to contend that history is being made if no one either knows or cares.

But perhaps the more substantive point is that the issues raised by the likes of Boccardi and Dowell put a series of question marks against the kind of moral character that is realized and required within the field of journalistic practice. Quite simply, the opposition within the field between the objective and the sensationalist camps means that the determination of character is fundamentally conflictual. Boccardi and Dowell tend to assume that the conflict can be overcome in the practice of the individual journalist all the time that she or he allows the inclinations and tendencies of the one camp to be tempered by the other. However, this neat resolution of the problem works only if objective and sensationalist journalism can be reconciled. What if they cannot? What if the field of journalistic production is irrevocably split between two irreconcilable definitions of what constitutes the good of this particular practice? This is a point that the likes of Boccardi and Dowell do not confront.

The distinct possibility of such an irreconcilable difference is implicit to MacIntyre's understanding of goods as being internal to practices. One of the corollaries of this position is that there is no point of arbitration between these different goods (between, in this case, the goods of objective reporting and sensational human interest reporting). At best there can only be a mutual lack of understanding of the opposite position. But that degree of tolerance towards a different perspective upon what it is that constitutes good journalistic practice is likely to prevail only in those institutional contexts in which there is little or no competition over access to scarce resources (that is, in those contexts where market concerns are not dominant). That was indeed the situation which existed in Britain until John Birt became the director-general of the BBC and committed the corporation to an attempt to secure a greater share of the audience in order to justify the case that funding should continue to be raised through a universal licence fee. Until then, the BBC and independent television were able to pursue different news agenda more or less in isolation from one another. That divide historically led to a situation in which the BBC was seen to practise the good of objectivity and impartiality whereas independent news sources were commonly identified as operating more in terms of criteria of human interest. But as soon as there is a struggle over access to a finite supply of scarce resources (and audience ratings can be identified as such a resource), the situation is radically transformed. Then, the competing positions come into conflict with one another in an attempt to secure and maintain access through broadcasting popular programmes and by trying to sign up the big celebrities of the day (as such, in Britain there is a relatively flourishing market between channels trying to attract the big name news presenters). In these ways, each broadcaster hopes to be able to maintain access to the scarce resources of audience share and market profile. As Bourdieu pointed out, those institutions which are best able to reflect and respond to the ever-changing demands of the market are the most likely to achieve a position of dominance. They will gradually become the referents of the good. The tensions between rival conceptions of the good will not be transcended so much as managed through power relations and institutional processes.

This has implications for the nature and goods of journalistic practice. Instead of veering towards the middle ground between objectivity and human interest, practice will tend to fall back on to tried and tested formula which will secure audiences readily and quickly. In other words, the character of the journalist is subjected to a reorientation, away from a commitment to either (or both) of the positions within the field of practice and rather more towards the manipulation of the audience so that it will come to prefer one news source rather than another. And that in turn means that the report ceases to be an end in itself (the objective telling of history or the communication of a certain human interest) and, instead, it becomes a means to the end of securing resources. In MacIntyre's terms this means that the virtues of the journalistic field collapse into a condition of what he calls *emotivism*.

For MacIntyre, emotivism can be defined as the practice of preferences rather than goods (MacIntyre 1985: 11–14). It has been shown that the field of journalistic practice establishes standards of the good which, in their turn, justify claims about what ought to be done. Those claims about what *ought* to be done are the standpoint from which it thereby becomes possible to condemn as unethical that which *is* done. Within this field of practice, photographers or reporters do not simply do what they want to do. Instead, all practice is guided by ideals and commitments about what journalists ought to do on a given occasion and in certain circumstances. Yet those oughts become problematic in situations and circumstances that are marked by a struggle to maximize audience ratings. Not least, it is distinctly possible that the goods of objective journalism (such as fairness and impartiality) become incompatible with the demands for market share. After all, reports which go into great depth and detail are going to be costly to produce, they are going to eat into the time or space that is available and they are likely to lack any sensational aspect all the time that they try to offer an explanation of how the given event or problem has come to pass. The goods of objective journalistic practice are established by reference to certain ends which it is taken to be incumbent upon the individual to attempt to achieve. But if the media institution is engaged in a struggle for access to scarce resources, journalistic practice ceases to be an end in itself and, on the contrary, it becomes a means to some end that is external to it. The journalistic character has to be transformed. The journalist has to stop claiming to be the objective enquirer after truth and instead that character has to be one which is able to manipulate the audience and other scarce resources so that their availability is maximized. Consequently, even though the field of journalistic production is split between two opposing camps, broader contextual issues tend to lead to the emergence of a narrow range of journalistic productions and practices around the concern to manipulate access to resources rather than in the name of any ostensibly greater value.

This tension, and indeed the relationship between compassion fatigue and journalistic practice, has been highlighted by Susan D. Moeller. Her book, *Compassion Fatigue* (Moeller 1999), is somewhat problematic because it never really defines what the phrase means (Moeller's text relies on assertion and repetition in order to make the phrase 'compassion fatigue' work as anything approaching an analytic concept). However, she does offer evidence which supports the argument about a restriction of journalistic productions and an increasing predictability about its features. According to Moeller, compassion fatigue is the nub of the short attention span and boredom that media audiences seem to have in relation to news reports. But she sees this audience reaction as an effect rather than a cause. The cause of compassion fatigue, according to Moeller, lies elsewhere, in the nature and the context of contemporary journalistic practice.

A number of Moeller's bullet points for explaining the phenomenon of compassion fatigue are worth drawing out since they add a little detail to the argument which is being constructed here, namely that the virtues of journalistic practice and, more specifically, the character types of objectivity and sensationalism have been distorted by competition for scarce resources and overlain with a project of manipulation. First, Moeller says that, 'Compassion fatigue reinforces simplistic, formulaic coverage. If images of starving babies worked in the past to capture attention for a complex crisis of war, refugees and famine, then starving babies will headline the next difficult crisis'. Second, 'To forestall the I've-seen-it-before syndrome, journalists reject events that aren't more dramatic or more lethal than their predecessors. Or, through a choice of language and images, the newest event is represented as being more extreme or deadly or risky than a similar past situation'. Third, Moeller says that, 'compassion fatigue tempts journalists to find ever more sensational tidbits in stories to retain the attention of their audience' and, finally, it 'encourages the media to move on to other stories once the range of possibilities of coverage have been exhausted so that boredom doesn't set in' (Moeller 1999: 2). To a very significant extent, the bulk of Moeller's book is little more than an extension, illustration and confirmation of these opening contentions. She rather tends to assume what she really needs to explain.

It is unsurprising that those journalists who identify themselves as the practitioners of an internal good of sufficiency to the unique event and, therefore, in terms of the role of the virtuous character, find these kinds of constraints to be prejudicial to the integrity of their work. For example, at a conference organized by the Reuters Foundation in 1998, the BBC journalist George Alagiah spoke about the emergence of 'template reporting' which 'implies that there is a formulaic way of reporting a humanitarian crisis'. Now Alagiah wants to challenge the idea that it is possible to identify any template for the coverage of humanitarian crises such as famine or war. He contends that it is the role of the journalist to use stock phrases or imagery (which allow the rapid communication of the issue) in new and different ways according to his or her values: 'the truth of the matter is that it's what the reporter does in between those ingredients that makes it a report, makes it powerful, makes it informative. And if you don't have a sense of commitment, a sense of attachment to what you're seeing, you'll never be able to write it'. The problem is, however, that Alagiah finds it extremely easy to describe the 'ingredients' of the 'template' and, indeed, when he ticks them off it is almost possible to picture the report in our mind's eye. In other words, even as Alagiah seeks to challenge the hold of template reporting, he actually manages to indicate how pervasive it is: 'You've got to have the emaciated child, preferably crying; you've got to have a feeding centre where mothers with sunken breasts are trying to calm their children; you've got to have an aid worker, usually white, usually a woman who is working against the odds and yet has time to come and tell us, the reporter and the audience, how difficult it all is' (Alagiah 1998).

According to Alagiah the only way the journalist can challenge the grip of the template is by lapsing into a mode of reporting which emphasizes an emotional engagement with the suffering rather than which seeks to give the facts of what is happening. In that way, Alagiah seems to believe that the deadness of familiarity and convention can be reinvigorated. What is interesting is the way that Alagiah sets up a dualism in the ways of reporting suffering which reflects the account of the opposition in the field of journalistic practice that this chapter has sought to develop by drawing out themes from Bourdieu. Alagiah sets up a contrast between what he terms 'evocative' and 'diagnostic' journalism. What Alagiah calls 'diagnostic reporting' resonates with the objective values which Bourdieu identifies as one of sites in the field of journalistic practice. Alagiah says that, 'To be diagnostic is to deconstruct the problem, analyse its causes, portray the context in which the story is taking place' (Alagiah 1998). This is, perhaps, a less loaded depiction of Martin Bell's 'bystander's journalism'.

Meanwhile, Alagiah contends that 'evocative' reporting expresses the ethical claim for the journalist that, 'when I'm in the field, a part of me must be like a viewer. I must feel the same sense of shock, of shame, as they would and find a way to express those feelings . . . there ought to be a bond between the reporter and the viewer'. In a direct rejection of the logic of the argument about compassion fatigue which is developed by Janine di Giovanni, Alagiah says that, 'I must never, ever, allow myself to become so punch-drunk that I'm no longer horrified by what I see' (Alagiah 1998). This is a rejection and a rebuttal of di Giovanni's argument for the simple reason that, insofar as Alagiah is an immensely experienced journalist, he should (by di Giovanni's account) have reached the stage at which he simply passes the starving by and cannot possibly feel a sense of horror because he feels bored instead. Yet Alagiah gives another justification for this kind of 'evocative' reporting. He says that it is justifiable because it tackles the question of 'how do you make people care?' He answers: 'A war in Europe matters because perhaps British troops, British citizens, may become involved. But how many actually care without prompting if, for example, the Angolans keep on fighting for another twenty years? The reporter has to find a way of personalising the experience' (Alagiah 1998). It is worth noting that this personalization of the issue turns the journalist into the representative of the audience, thereby opening up a space in which the problem of compassion fatigue can be found. That problem is one of what does it mean for the journalist when the audience evidently fails to share her or his sense of shock and horror?

Alagiah is able to pull together 'diagnostic' and 'evocative' reporting only by giving a primacy to the latter but, in asserting that primacy, he radically changes the nature and the meaning of journalistic practice itself. The implication of Alagiah's case is that, in appealing to the audience on the basis of some presumption of a shared moral sensibility, it becomes the role and the purpose of the journalist to tell the members of the audience how they would feel if they could see, hear and smell all that the journalist is able to sense. In other words the journalist stops being the communicator of an event and, instead, lapses into the very different role of telling others what they ought to be feeling and thinking about this. This means that journalists subordinate the virtues of either and both objectivity and sensationalism and, instead, elevate to the pedestal of the measurement of journalistic excellence, their ability to manipulate the feelings of others. It is also worth noting that Alagiah presents the resolution of the distinction between evocative and diagnostic reporting as a matter of the choice that is made by the journalist. He presents it as a *preference*. The actual suffering becomes a means to an end that is entirely and wholly external to it. It is but a short step to the situation in which, 'We remember the names of those who report . . . [wars] – John Simpson, Kate Adie, Robert Fisk – far more readily than we remember the names of the generals who fought them' (Worsthorne 1999: 33).

Conclusion

Compassion fatigue can be defined as the bad faith which emerges out of the opposition in the field of journalistic production when the practices and the goods that it justifies and legitimizes are placed in a situation of competition for scarce resources. 'Bad faith' here refers to the subjective feeling on the part of the photographer or the reporter that they have failed to fulfil the demands and the compulsions of the goods which are internal to the field journalistic practice, have turned away from that field itself and have, instead, turned into a manipulator. As soon as journalistic production is motivated by manipulation it cannot possibly be motivated by and oriented towards the realization of the virtues which are internal to the field of production (however contradictory those virtues might be). By their own criteria of excellence and legitimacy, therefore, individual journalists come to identify their own practice with a certain insufficiency, inadequacy and lack.

It is taken to be failing to achieve what was intended. This sense is internalized by the subjects of the field of journalistic production precisely because they cannot possibly arbitrate between the competing demands that are made of them and neither can they step outside of the field of production without ceasing to be journalists as such.

These are the sociological causes of what is called compassion fatigue, but the phrase also refers to an empirical problem. If journalists identify themselves as the representative of the audience (and that identification emerges for sociological reasons and not simply because of a desire for personal self-aggrandizement), they have to assume that the audience ought to feel exactly what the journalist feels when confronted with suffering and misery. Yet that degree of imitation is a rare occurrence. It means that if journalists do not want to challenge the presumption of a universalized common humanity, which links themselves, the victims and the audiences, then they must blame the discrepancy between what they feel and what the audience seems to feel on their own failure to communicate.

The irony is, however, that all of this casts considerable doubt on the validity of any conception of journalistic compassion fatigue. One of the implications of this chapter has been that it is absolutely wrong to identify some general psychological state which typifies all contemporary journalistic practice. It is simply not the case that all journalists have reached a state in which they have completely and decisively 'switched off' from feeling any bond of empathy with the suffering of another. If that were the case, few journalists and fewer commentators upon journalistic practice would be worrying about something called 'compassion fatigue'. Instead, it is best to approach 'compassion fatigue' as a more or less inaccurate but nevertheless extremely vibrant and accessible label through which a number of commentators struggle to come to terms with the tensions and oppositions within journalism which are thrown up by the relationships of the field of journalistic practice. Compassion fatigue is the inappropriate label which is used in order to try to develop some appreciation for and statement of the virtues of journalistic practice in a broader context in which that practice – just like the journalistic field – is marked by a quest for access to scarce resources rather more than it is marked by concerns to develop a repertoire of moral characters which might offer role models for the engagement of the individual with others.

Note

1 Throughout this discussion, I continue to use the word 'objectivity' when discussing certain journalistic practice and production. I am of course aware of the

voluminous and significant academic literature which would drastically undermine the contention that any journalistic practice or production can ever be called truly 'objective' (that is to say, an undistorted and straight, unmediated, account, representation or explanation of what 'really happened'). However, my point is a different one. The point I am wanting to make is that certain significant journalistic practice and production upholds a commitment to the virtues of objectivity and impartiality. It is that commitment which it is my concern to examine and, from this point of view, the relationship of media production to 'reality' or 'truth' is an entirely separate issue. For a relevant discussion of some of the ethical issues surrounding objectivity, see Allan (1999) and Kieran (1998).

Further reading

Alagiah, G. (1998) Contribution to the conference, Dispatches from Disaster Zones: Reporting Humanitarian Disasters, held in London 27–28 May. Transcript available at http: //www.alertnet.org

Bell, M. (1996b) Conflict of interest, *The Guardian*, 11 July: 19.

Bourdieu, P. (1998) *On Television and Journalism*. (Trans. P. Parkhurst Ferguson.) London: Pluto.

di Giovanni, J. (1994) Tired moving of the pictures: Bosnia and Rwanda, *Sunday Times*, 14 August: 10/8.

Girardet, E.R. (ed.) (1995) *Somalia, Rwanda, and Beyond: The Role of the International Media in Wars and Humanitarian Crises*. Dublin: Crosslines.

Kieran, M. (1998) Objectivity, impartiality and good journalism, in M. Kieran (ed.) *Media Ethics*. London: Routledge.

Moeller, S.D. (1999) *Compassion Fatigue: How the Media Sell Disease, Famine, War and Death*. New York: Routledge.

THE COMPASSION
OF THE AUDIENCE

Introduction

Chapter 2 explored some of the issues that are raised for the practice of journalistic production by the debate about compassion fatigue. It was suggested that journalistic practice is organized around two competing logics and that this competition and indeed conflict creates subjective difficulties for photographers and reporters. These professionals are torn between the demands of objectivity and the demands of the market. They are torn in such a way that, whether they choose one option or the other or whether they struggle to strike some happy medium, they are nevertheless confronted with the feeling that however good their product and production might be, it is never quite good enough. There is always a competing definition of good journalistic practice that needs to be taken into account. Or, in the case of those journalists who attempt to occupy the middle ground between the outright demands of objectivity and the market, there are always two standards of the excellent towards which the particular report or representation fails to approximate.

Further, it was proposed that journalists can overcome these conflicts and contradictions – and it must be emphasized that they are of a sociological nature and not reducible to individual idiosyncrasies and neuroses – only to the extent that they try to define themselves as the representatives of the audience. But, in that case, the journalists are confronted with the problem of judgement of how to make sense of those instances when the audience evidently does not respond to the report of suffering and misery with all of the intensity and sense of outrage that the journalists themselves felt. This is the problem that is resolved by the concept of compassion fatigue. The photographers and reporters take the contradictions of the field of journalistic production onto themselves, and explain the gap between their own feelings and the responses of the audience as an effect of their own moral exhaustion. They judge themselves as failing.

It is possible, therefore, to talk about an *ethics* of the journalistic field. By that token, it is also possible to identify one of the key sites of divergence between the moral horizons of photographers and reporters on the one hand, and the audience of the productions on the other. The journalistic field is a context in which individuals are educated in the virtues of what constitutes 'good practice'. As we have seen, those virtues might well be organized around two contradictory logics, but nevertheless the point remains that it is possible for photographers and reporters to organize their action in terms of reasonably clear standards of the good which are internal to the journalistic field itself. Consequently, the subjects of the field of journalistic practice can be identified in principle as men and women of virtue. The situation is by no means the same when the focus of attention turns to the audience.

The meaning of the audience

When I use the word 'audience' I do so in a fairly straightforward – some might say simplistic – manner. It is good enough for the purposes of this discussion to define the audience as, simply, the imagined unity which is constituted by and of those who read newspapers which have some commonality of content and those who listen to or watch the same radio or television broadcasts. Of course, the constituencies of the newspaper readers and the broadcast listeners and viewers are not mutually exclusive. This is a very simple definition, but it does have a degree of conceptual purchase that is perfectly sufficient for us.

First, this definition makes the point that the concept of the audience is a theoretical abstraction. In the terms of sociological methodology, the audience can be identified and interpreted as an ideal type: 'To this extent, the construction is merely a technical aid which facilitates a more lucid arrangement and terminology' (Weber 1948: 324). This ideal type can be used as the object of analysis because it manages to pull together a variety of different, but nevertheless comparable and not contradictory, social and cultural relationships and practices into something approaching a coherent whole. As Max Weber, the main exemplar of the method of the ideal type, wrote: 'Thus, for substantive reasons, we may hope to facilitate the presentation of an otherwise immensely multifarious subject matter by expediently constructed rational types'. He went on: 'To do this we must prepare and emphasise the internally most "consistent" forms of practical conduct that can be deduced from fixed and given presuppositions' (Weber 1948: 324). It follows that the discussion of the audience which is going to be developed here is fully aware of empirical social and cultural relationships and practices, but the totality and the unity of those relationships and practices is a methodological construction and clarification. It is not a straightforward property of the empirical, objective, world itself.

Second, the definition makes it clear that it is possible to construct an ideal type of the audience only insofar as it is in the first instance possible to identify a range of relationships and practices that are common and distinguishable. This is why it is important to stress the point that the definition of the audience must include an emphasis upon press and broadcasting and, moreover, upon the continuities of those different media. These media can be identified as continuous, common and distinguishable to the extent that they bring an 'out there' into the spatial and imaginative 'in here' from which action might subsequently ensue. The audience is recognizable *as* an audience on the basis of the role that is played by the media in the constitution of the possibility of particular types of social and cultural imagination and practice.

Third, in that the concept of the audience refers to a type of imagination and practice that is fundamentally common (that is to say, not individual), it also contains a social dimension. No one of us is the only person who reads newspapers or who watches television; other people do the same things as well. Or, to put this claim more strongly, it might be said that the audience is a *social* constituency. And, as a social constituency, it engages in social action. But that comment begs the question of the meaning of the term 'social action'. Weber says that, 'Social action, which includes both failure to act and passive acquiescence, may be oriented to the past, present, or expected future behavior of others'. Weber continues: 'The "others" may be individual persons, and may be known to the actor as such, or may constitute an indefinite plurality and may be entirely unknown as individuals' (Weber 1968: 22).

It is important to fasten on to the point that Weber is seeking to define *social action* rather than simply *action*. In other words, some action can be labelled *non-social*. Weber establishes an important difference between the two. He identifies social action as being 'confined to cases where the actor's behavior is meaningfully oriented to that of others' (Weber 1968: 23), while action can be labelled as non-social, 'if it is oriented solely to the behavior of inanimate objects'. Action is also non-social if it is entirely self-focused, if it is entirely self-centred. In this context, Weber says that, in sociological terms at least, 'For example, religious behavior is not social if it is simply a matter of contemplation or of solitary prayer. The economic activity of an individual is social only if it takes account of the behavior of someone else' (Weber 1968: 22). Similarly, a hypothetical individual who reads the newspaper and watches television entirely on their own and without any communication of any sort with others, is engaging in action, not *social* action. Meanwhile, to the extent that journalists are always and necessarily orienting their action towards others, they are always engaging in social action, not just action.

Social action means taking others into account, regardless of whether those others are recognizable and known individuals or, in principle, simply indeterminate others who are identified as being compellingly significant by the actor. To the extent that the concept of the audience implies *social action*, and to the extent that social action means *taking others into account*, it can be concluded that the audience is a *moral constituency*. Of course, the crucial point which needs to be added to these claims is that the others who are taken into account by the audience are of at least two different orders. The others can be fellow members of the audience (such as those who share the domestic sphere of media use or those with whom one discusses what has been read or seen) or those others can be the suffering and miserable on the page or screen, towards whom the members of the audience might in principle feel themselves to have some obligation to uphold or duty to perform. (This interpretation of morality as social action is derived from Tester 1999b.)

If it is accepted that the audience can be interpreted as a moral constituency, it becomes possible to develop the discussion of compassion fatigue in a fairly substantial way. The nub of the debate about compassion fatigue becomes a question about the fate of social action.

In Chapter 2, compassion fatigue was seen as a problem for the photographers and reporters who operate within and in terms of the field of journalistic practice. That identification of compassion fatigue with journalists might well have seemed somewhat curious since, in its more common usage, compassion fatigue is invariably linked to audiences who are, the argument runs, worn out by so much suffering and misery. Compassion fatigue is more usually identified as a *public* not a *professional* problem. This emphasis on the public is clear in the little existing academic literature about compassion fatigue (and, as we saw in Chapter 2, the connection of compassion to the public is also stressed by Natan Sznaider). For example, one of the more significant pieces of literature states that, 'In recent years . . . the term has been used . . . in the popular press and in philanthropic and fund-raising circles, to describe . . . a numbing of public concern toward social problems'.

Debate about the erstwhile phenomenon tends to 'portray a public grown weary of unrelenting media coverage of human tragedy and ubiquitous fund-raising appeals'. Whenever talk turns to compassion fatigue, implicitly the case is being made that the development of this weariness is worrying and unacceptable (Kinnick *et al.* 1996: 687).

According to the important study by Katherine N. Kinnick, Dean M. Krugman and Glen T. Cameron, compassion fatigue has arisen as a consequence of a combination of the ubiquity of the media in contemporary social and cultural relationships along with their values of production. They say that: 'Characteristics of the mass media which would be expected to contribute to compassion fatigue include its ubiquity in everyday life and journalistic news values which influence portrayals of social problems'. On the first point, ubiquity, Kinnick *et al.* (1996) suggest that the media pervade contemporary life and, moreover, that each media channel tends to follow the lead of its competitors. No media source wishes to go too far out on a limb, in case existing audiences and markets are lost. According to Kinnick *et al.*, this means that bad news itself becomes pervasive (because it is more amenable to sensationalization) and there is a 'normalization of social problems'. On the second point, news values, Kinnick *et al.* suggest that four tendencies in current news practice are relevant to the issue of compassion fatigue. First, there is an emphasis upon the sensational (that is, a preference for conflict and violence). The second factor is the domination of 'bad news' which is 'exacerbated by the tendency of the media to present problems but not their solutions, contributing to feelings of inefficacy among media consumers'. Third, 'The result of this failure to provide solutions is that the media overwhelm people . . . Feelings of inefficacy may constrain information seeking and interpersonal communication'. Finally, 'the media often fail to provide context or in-depth coverage of social problems through the coverage of events and not necessarily their meanings' (all quotations from Kinnick *et al.* 1996: 690; compare these points to the causes of compassion fatigue outlined in Moeller 1999).

Kinnick, Krugman and Cameron explored the validity of these possible causes of compassion fatigue through a qualitative research project which sought to tabulate the responses of 316 residents of Atlanta to a number of standard questions. On the basis of this sample population, the research reached three conclusions.

First, it was concluded that, 'compassion fatigue is issue-dependent'. It was found that the issues of AIDS and homelessness 'did not arouse respondents' concern to nearly the same degree as violent crime and child abuse'. Kinnick *et al.* speculated that this was because most respondents were able to distance themselves from the issues of AIDS and homelessness. They could disengage from these issues in a way that they could not when the focus of concern was violent crime and child abuse. Here, the point is that the latter two issues are felt to be relevant to everyone whereas, 'for issues like homelessness and AIDS' there are 'perceptions that victims are to blame for their situations' (Kinnick *et al.* 1996: 702). It is possible to believe that homelessness and AIDS happen to 'people like them' whereas crime and child abuse happens to 'people like us' because of 'people like them'.

Second, it was concluded that, 'compassion fatigue is an individual, multi-dimensional phenomenon'. What this means is that individuals will respond to pervasive coverage of an issue or a problem in a variety of ways. There is no monolithic cause or pattern to compassion fatigue. It varies. It is in this context that Kinnick *et al.* report that, 'for those who are initially disinterested or biased against victims of a social problem, pervasive media coverage likely serves to entrench negative feelings towards victims and foster desensitization' (a kind of 'oh, them again' factor). Meanwhile, those who are initially sympathetic will tend to have a number of responses as the media coverage continues. It 'may foster disinterest based on boredom . . . it may foster frustration and emotional desensitization when it appears that nothing can be done, or that the victims' own behavior is to blame for their situations'. And yet, 'for others, it may increase sensitivity toward the issue in an optimal way that encourages empathy with victims. And for a final group . . . coverage of some social problems may contribute to empathic distress at a level sufficient to motivate avoidance of topics which are emotionally draining' (Kinnick *et al.* 1996: 702–3).

Third, Kinnick, Krugman and Cameron concluded somewhat uncontroversially that, 'The media play a primary role in the development of compassion fatigue'. They go on to state that the media have this impact in two ways: 'by providing content that serves as aversive stimuli, prompting avoidance strategies; and by fostering desensitization to social problems through redundant and predominantly negative messages which reach the point of saturation' (Kinnick *et al.* 1996: 703). In other words, the media enhance and stimulate feelings of compassion fatigue because they make the audience seek to avoid certain issues and, moreover, because they lead the audience to reach the conclusion that nothing can be done about this problem and, quite possibly, about any other problem as well.

Interestingly, these empirical findings seem to bear out some of the themes which Michael Ignatieff developed in his more speculative essay about the moral significance of television. Ignatieff argues that by themselves television pictures of suffering cannot enforce a definite meaning, rather they can only 'instantiate' a moral claim (that is, they only press a moral meaning) to the extent that, 'those who watch understand themselves to be potentially under obligation to those they see' (Ignatieff 1998: 12). He believes that this obligation is rooted in the historical ideal of moral universalism. Yet, even as television can be read as an agent of the propagation of a rather lofty ideal of moral universalism, it also manages to depoliticize suffering. Consequently, the suffering of others tends to become more like a natural event to which we need to respond rather than a political event about which something preemptive might have been done. It might be said that media coverage means that we become aware of the killers only after they have killed, since the absence of suffering is not news.

Ignatieff says that, 'television images are more effective at presenting consequences than in exploring intentions; more adept at pointing to the corpses than in explaining why violence may, in certain places, pay so well'. For Ignatieff this tendency of television is directly responsible for the emergence of what he calls 'one of the dangerous cultural moods of our time', the belief that the world is so out of control and so terrible that all we can do is disengage from it (Ignatieff 1998: 25; compare Bourdieu 1998: 7–8).

Ignatieff emphasizes the role of the genre of television news in this paradoxical situation of the enhancement of moral empathy going hand-in-hand with what amounts to a disengagement from the world. He rightly points to the fact that television news tends to be full of the suffering of others in such a way that any single instance of horror becomes rather banal, and he continues to suggest that the format of television news means that there emerges a serious gap between the moral meaning of suffering and the moment of the consumption of the pictures or the report. Ignatieff says that one of the very minimum requirements if we are to engage with the suffering of others is that we spend time with them, 'enough time to pierce the carapace of self-absorption and estrangement that separates us from the moral world of others' (Ignatieff 1998: 29). This is precisely what television news does *not* permit and, by the logical extension of Ignatieff's argument, it can be concluded that, for him, all television news does permit, even as and when it tells of the most terrible suffering, is the self-absorption of the viewer. He writes that, 'the news makes it impossible to attend to what one has seen. In the end, one sees only the news, its personalities, its rules of selection and suppression, its authoritative voice' (Ignatieff 1998: 30). In a not dissimilar vein, Bauman has written about how television enables 'jumping in and out of foreign spaces with a speed much beyond the capacity of supersonic jets and cosmic rockets' (Bauman 1998: 77). Needless to say, those who suffer do not have this ability to escape and evade. That is one of the meanings of suffering.

It is possible to read the analysis of compassion fatigue that Kinnick, Krugman and Cameron develop as well as Ignatieff's more essayistic claims, in terms of the ideal type of the audience which has been sketched here. In these terms, compassion fatigue comes to stand for the collapse or denial on the part of the audience of a commitment to the human otherness of those who are reported and represented. The denial is a product of the mixture of boredom, desensitization, negative feelings and emotional draining that Kinnick *et al.* identify. Moreover, following from Ignatieff, these feelings can themselves be identified as a consequence of the genre of television news, which allows the audience to spend no time with the suffering and misery of others, making it instead a fleeting concern. All of this means that the sufferers cease to be others towards whom the individual actors need to orient themselves and, instead, the other becomes nothing more than a perennial victim and potential threat who is beyond help and hope. Consequently, there is a breakdown of social action (because the other ceases to be identified as human and instead becomes little more than a thing that is consigned to pain) and, by extension, a disintegration of the moral bond that might link the audience to those indefinite others about whom what they see and read is all that they know. Moral universalism seems to offer no obstacle to apathy.

However, in the light of the study and the essay, it does become reasonable to propose that, just like the subjects of the field of journalistic practice, the audience can be identified with the possibility of morality. Both indicate that the audience *can* act in orientation towards others (that is to say, *can* care) and, therefore, that social action is *possible*. (However, great care needs to be taken to avoid falling into the methodological fallacy of proposing that because social action is possible it therefore happens. Statements of theoretical possibility are not identical with, and must not be confused with, statements about empirical occurrence. Some studies of the purported strategies of resistance of audiences forget this point.) Therefore, there is a normative problem when the other comes to lack the ability to make the audience orient itself towards suffering and misery. But, unlike the subjects of the field of journalistic practice, it cannot be concluded that the audience is therefore possessed of an *ethical* horizon or sensibility. There is no reason to expect the audience necessarily to feel that any breakdown of an orientation towards the other represents a denial of what *ought* to be done. The audience does not contain the ethical awareness that would make statements of the ought binding or the practices of virtue possible. Of course, I am not saying that the individual members of the audience do not recognize to some extent or another the ethical positions which are being adopted in the field of journalistic production. What I am saying is that there is no reason to assume that those claims or positions have any great relevance for the members of the audience. I am not making a claim about ethical *ignorance*; I am making a claim about ethical *confusion*.

This point needs clarification. I am *not* saying that the individual actors who constitute the audience are without ethical horizons and neither am I saying that they cannot be men and women of virtue. They can be insofar as they organize the entirety of their social and cultural practice in terms of one specific context of action that has its own internal good. To this extent, all social actors are able to consider themselves as being more or less ethical. What I *am* saying is that the media themselves offer no such internal good because they are actually corrosive of internal goods. This is because the media communicate a variety of different ethical positions and present them all as more or less equal and equivalent in such a way that the good becomes something about which it is impossible to be certain or confident. And it is in that light that it is possible to contend that the audience is without an ethical dimension. This is precisely the reason why some commentators have called for 'virtue in media use' (Lubbe 1996: 59) and also why their calls are so likely to fall upon deaf ears. The individual actors who together constitute the audience are only capable of virtue and of being ethical insofar as they are not *just* members of the audience.

How can it be possible to claim that the audience is without an ethical dimension and that the media are incapable of generating any practices of virtue? To explore that issue, attention needs to be paid to the broad social and historical context within which the individuals whose actions are pulled together by and within the ideal type of the audience are situated.

Incommensurability and the media

The audience does not have a definite ethical dimension because contemporary social and cultural relationships are marked and characterized by a situation of ethical **incommensurability**. As with the understanding of virtue which was central to the discussion of journalistic practice in Chapter 2, the concept of ethical incommensurability is derived from the work of the moral philosopher Alasdair MacIntyre. What we need to do now is think about MacIntyre's work in a little more detail, provide examples to illustrate it and, finally, move on to see what light it might cast upon our question of the relationship between compassion, morality and the media.

MacIntyre contends that contemporary debate about issues such as warfare, abortion and access to education and health care are typified by disagreements and disputes between a number of competing perspectives. Each of these perspectives on the issue at hand is consistent and coherent in its own terms, 'But the rival premises are such that we possess no rational way of weighing the claims of one as against another'. MacIntyre continues: 'For each premise employs some quite different normative or evaluative concept from the others, so that claims made upon us are of quite different kinds' (MacIntyre 1985: 8).

A good illustration of what MacIntyre is getting at is provided by the debate about abortion and, in particular, the way in which that debate has been polarized between the so-called 'pro-life' and 'pro-choice' positions. Now, each position is logical and consistent taken on its own terms. However, the premises from which they commence are radically different. For example, 'pro-life' positions contend that human life is sacrosanct irrespective of its developmental stage or whether it is inside the womb or outside. By this argument abortion is absolutely wrong. Meanwhile 'pro-choice' positions contend that a woman has a right to control her own body and fertility and that a foetus cannot claim, or be accorded, any more powerful rights until such time as it is fully capable of an independent existence. By this argument, abortion can be perfectly acceptable. Each position begins from an initial premise which is in contradiction to that of the other position. It is impossible for us to judge rationally between the initial premises or to make an objective statement about the rival claims that they make upon us. Of course, it could be objected that there is no incommensurability in the abortion debate because both positions agree that life is sacrosanct and must not be harmed. But that objection is invalid for the simple reason that it is impossible to reach agreement about the meaning of the word 'life'.

A similar situation characterizes the widespread debate about whether new drugs should be tested on live animals before they are unleashed upon humans. For one side in the debate it would be completely reckless and foolhardy to subject humans to drugs which have not been tested fully and thoroughly. After all, the drugs might have terrible and unexpected side-effects which might, possibly, be far more painful than the initial illness. For this side in the debate, research on living animals is an absolutely necessary technique which will enable us to make more or less informed calculations about the riskiness of using new drugs. The animals are seen as tools which can be used for human ends which are, themselves, given a greater moral significance and weighting than any interests or rights that the rats or the monkeys might themselves possess or make. However, for the other side in the debate, such an argument is little more than unethical 'speciesism' which must be resisted and overthrown at every opportunity. For this side in the debate, the rats and the monkeys in laboratories have interests or rights in ways which are morally identical to the interests of rights of humans. To ignore those interests or rights, or to pretend that the animals are less significant simply because they are not human, is to replace ethics and morality with dull power and oppression. From this side of the debate it is simply grotesque and wrong to treat animals in a way which would not be coun-tenanced if the living creature were another human being.

The point is that, taken on their own terms, each side of the debate builds up a logical argument from an initial premise which is incompatible with the initial premise of the competitor position. For example, those who defend live experiments are likely to argue that animals are physically similar to humans and yet morally different such that they can be used for human ends in order to supply scientifically valid knowledge. Meanwhile, those who attack live experimentation are likely to argue that humans and animals are physically similar to such an extent that it is simply wrong to treat them as means to human ends or to pretend that what animals might want or need is less important than the claims that are made by humans. Neither initial premise can really come to terms with the other. Consequently, the two sides in the debate are not talking *to* one another; they are talking *past* one another.

The positions are incommensurable: 'We know how to construct valid arguments using one set of premises or another, but we don't know how to appraise the significance of the concepts used in any given argument with-out begging the question' (Stout 1988: 210). The question that is left beg-ging is precisely that of the significance and validity of our premises. As MacIntyre would have us appreciate, there is actually no way of rationally arbitrating between the different premises and saying that the one is truly ethical rather than the other. For MacIntyre, this means that moral debate and discourse is currently marked by a certain 'shrillness' and 'interminabil-ity' (MacIntyre 1985: 8). Debate turns into disagreement, and disagreement becomes increasingly vitriolic if not, in fact, violent (witness what has hap-pened to the abortion debate in the United States or to the debate about animal rights in Britain).

The consequence of the incommensurability of ethical positions is that there is an absence of any social and cultural consensus over statements and practices of what ought to be done. To continue with one of our examples, think of the case of a doctor who carries out abortions. Is that doctor respecting the rights of women or is the doctor murdering baby humans? The answer to the question, and the kinds of practice in relation to the abor-tion debate which would ensue from whatever answer is given, depends upon one's initial premises. And between the premises it is impossible ration-ally to judge. A similar question can be asked of audiences: given that any individual social actor can only provide a finite amount of sustenance to the suffering and the miserable, who should be helped? The children living in poverty in the city one hundred miles away or the refugees who have been raped and orphaned? Once again, it is impossible rationally to arbitrate between the competing claims. It is possible to develop completely compelling and logically coherent arguments which uphold the demands of the children or the refugees, but it is impossible to decide between those competing arguments. It is impossible to say what ought to be done and, therefore, it is impossible to make any decisive and consensually valid ethical judgements.

According to MacIntyre, the situation of incommensurability has arisen as the result of various factors. They range from the internal difficulties of philosophical argumentation, to the impact of broad social and cultural processes such as secularization (which he believes involves a multiplication of ethical positions in the wake of the collapse of a general commitment to a theological system of ethics; MacIntyre 1967) and, implicitly rather than by express statement, to the impact of liberal democratic political arrangements which presuppose and bolster disagreement over initial premises. Yet if the net of analysis is cast beyond the shores of MacIntyre, it becomes clear that this account of ethical incommensurability is not too startling. Classical sociologists like Marx, Durkheim, Simmel and Weber would have probably found much to support in the general story that MacIntyre tells. For example, a recurrent theme in Marx's corpus of work is the problem of the split of universal aspirations and human capacities between the incommensurable principles of bourgeois and proletarian ethics (see in particular Marx and Engels 1942). A little later, Durkheim was keenly aware that the division of labour meant that universal ethical positions are absent from industrialized societies and that, instead, different social classes and groups are associated with their own particular premises and therefore judgements of what ought to be done (Durkheim 1984). Equally, Max Weber's essays on the vocations of science and politics can be read as exegeses on the problem of virtue in circumstances in which it is impossible to know for sure what ought to be done (Weber 1948).

Now, MacIntyre rather restricts the analysis of incommensurability to the modes and style of moral discourse. That is why his book *After Virtue* tends to devote most of its attention to the trials and tribulations of philosophers and moralists. However, the fact that classical sociology can be interpreted as containing themes and perspectives which rest very easily with some of the claims that MacIntyre makes, demonstrates that the analysis of incommensurability can be broadened and identified as a manifestation of *social* processes.

Media and character

Two of the more famous and profound studies of contemporary American social life can help us understand the role of the media in the exacerbation of incommensurability. These studies are David Riesman's book *The Lonely Crowd* and the book *Habits of the Heart*, which was written by Robert Bellah and his colleagues in the early 1980s (Riesman 1960; Bellah *et al.* 1986). Of course, it could be objected that these studies are of an entirely local usefulness given that they are about America. But that would be to underestimate the depth of their findings. Although the regional specificity of Riesman and Bellah has to be recognized, it also has to be appreciated that much of what they say seems to be valid for the understanding of other places, such as Britain. It is to *Habits of the Heart* that we turn first. What does that study have to say about the implications for ethics of the media?

Bellah and his co-authors raise themes and issues which leave us in no doubt that the media, and television in particular, do not simply represent the condition of the incommensurability of ethical claims and positions. Television attenuates the condition and, in so doing, it can be identified as playing no small part in exacerbating the 'shrillness' of so much contemporary moral discourse. They say of television that, 'it would be difficult to argue that there is any coherent ideology or overall message that it communicates'. Indeed, broadcasters 'do not support any clear set of beliefs or policies, yet they cast doubt on everything'. This is because the media, and to repeat, television especially, serve only to 'debunk' what was once taken for granted, respected and thought to possess integrity (Bellah *et al.* 1986: 279).

This contention immediately justifies the possibility that even though the claims that Bellah makes are based in a study of contemporary America, it nevertheless casts light on contemporary Britain. In particular, British commentators have argued that television has 'debunked' what were previously taken for granted ethical positions. The case was argued very powerfully by Jonathan Sacks in the immediate aftermath of the James Bulger murder. James Bulger was a 2-year-old boy who was murdered in February 1993 after being taken away from a shopping centre by two 10-year-old boys. They took James while his mother was in a shop and subsequently beat him to death beside a railway line. James was caught by video surveillance cameras, walking away hand-in-hand with the boys. According to Sacks (1995), the murder taught us all the lesson that the 'moral fabric' has been torn in Britain. And he contends that one of the causes of that tearing (which reveals the violence which lurks behind the scenes of social life) has been the way in which the media have destroyed the credibility of anyone towards whom we might look for an example of virtue and a demonstration of a moral character. Sacks wrote that, 'Politicians, religious leaders, the royal family, have all been mercilessly savaged until there is no one left whose word carries moral force . . . They have become figures of fun' (Sacks 1995: 14). Popular culture offers no replacements because the media are all too keen to tell all about the secrets and predilections of the rich and famous.

According to the Bellah study, television has a particularly deleterious impact upon ethics thanks to the genres of the soap opera and the situation comedy. *Habits of the Heart* claims that, 'both soaps and situation comedies are based on the same contrast: human decency versus brutal competitiveness for economic success . . . they both portray a world dominated by economic competition, where the only haven is a very small circle of warm personal relationships'. Consequently, both soaps and situation comedies alike reduce all questions of ethics to, 'the overwhelming dominance of material ambition' (Bellah *et al.* 1986: 280). This is a conclusion that one would also be led to expect by Marx and Durkheim, although the expectation is even greater for anyone who has read Georg Simmel's account of how the 'money system' destroys all values which cannot be quantified (Simmel 1997).

Bellah and his colleagues suggest that this kind of dull and simplistic ethic of possession and wealth is exacerbated by television because that medium stifles the possibility of any other sensibilities and horizons. They say that one of the main concerns of television broadcasters is to 'hook' the audience in order to get high ratings, but that since 'images and feelings are better communicated in this medium than ideas, television seeks to hold us . . . by the sheer succession of sensations. One sensation being as good as another, there is the implication that nothing makes any difference'. They go on to contend that, 'We switch from a quiz show to a situation comedy, to a bloody police drama, to a miniseries about celebrities, and with each click of the dial nothing remains' (Bellah *et al.* 1986: 280). It is easy to develop this point to propose that we (that is to say, the individual social actors who together constitute the methodological ideal type of the audience) switch from refugees in the Balkans to genocide in Africa and to climatic catastrophe in Asia – 'and with each click of the dial nothing remains'. If Bellah and his colleagues are right, the suffering and the misery that is seen on the screen, being experienced by others, is quite unable to impress itself upon the audience and, furthermore, it is highly improbable that the audience will experience any specific incident as being at all compelling. The social actors who together constitute the audience will not orient themselves towards others and any possibility of a moral bond between audience and the suffering and miserable others will be avoided. Once again, Ignatieff's moral universalism seems to be more than a little doubtful. Instead the wariness and caution of analysts like Finkielkraut and Bauman seems to be much more apposite.

Moreover, if it is valid to contend that genres such as soaps and situation comedies spread an ethic of material wealth and consumption, then it is likely that those who are seen on the screen to be suffering from want of material possessions will be interpreted as at least partially responsible for their own plight (and as we have already seen from Kinnick, Krugman and Cameron, the strategy of blaming the victim is one of the main ways in which orientations towards others can be avoided or denied). They will become members of that category of 'flawed consumers' which has been uncovered by Zygmunt Bauman. He writes in a way which compares with the Bellah study about how, in contemporary relationships (which Bauman identifies in this instance with consumer society), the practice and perhaps even the virtue of, 'A "happy life" is defined by catching the opportunities and letting slip but few or none at all, by catching the opportunities most talked about and thus most desired, and catching them no later than others, and preferably before others' (Bauman 1998b: 37). This is a happy life defined by material possession and aggressive acquisition. The dominant good is *to have*. It means that, 'the poor of a consumer society are people with no access to normal life, let alone to a happy one. In a consumer society . . . having no access to a happy or merely a normal life means to be consumers *manquées*, or flawed consumers'. Bauman continues to draw out the implication of this kind of identification of the poor as flawed. Their suffering and misery becomes their fault: 'And so the poor of a consumer society are socially defined, and self-defined, first and foremost as blemished, defective, faulty and deficient – in other words, inadequate – consumers' (Bauman 1998b: 38).

The implication of the points by Bellah and his colleagues is that television will only be experienced by its audience as making a moral demand when and if it is able to impress some kind of *sensation* of a demand. Yet Bauman seems to imply that the sensation is unlikely given that poverty and misery in a consumer society tend to be interpreted as the fault of the poor and miserable. At best, ethics will tend to be subjected to a general social and cultural shift away from ideals and aspirations and they will tend to become about feelings and emotions. Moreover, the kind of long term effort and personal commitment that is implied by any conception of virtue is quite incompatible with the demands and characteristics of television. According to Bellah and his colleagues, television does not – and indeed cannot – promote any kind of deferral or calculation and commitment over the long term. Rather it promotes and demands a fragmentation of experience in the search for the 'hook' of immediate sensation. They say that, 'Even aside from commercials, television style is singularly abrupt and jumpy, with many quick cuts to other scenes and other characters. Dialogue is reduced to clipped sentences. No one talks long enough to express anything complex. Depth of feeling, if it exists at all, has to be expressed in a word or a glance' (Bellah *et. al.* 1986: 280). The upshot is clear: 'Television is much more interested in how people feel than in what they think. What they think might separate us, but how they feel draws us together' (Bellah *et al.* 1986: 281).

It is worth considering that final point in more detail: what we feel draws us together. In MacIntyre's terms the discovery by Bellah and his colleagues of the significance of feeling is nothing other than confirmation of the parlous state of ethics in contemporary social and cultural relationships. The point is that if all claims about the good or the virtuous are taken to be at bottom about what we feel, then the chance of any rational debate about ethics and morality is terminally undermined. If the good and the right is what feels to me to be the good and the right, there is no necessary reason to imagine that you will share those feelings. And how could we possibly discuss our differences of opinion and how might we be able to come to some kind of agreement (even if it is only an agreement to differ)? We could not. Consequently, our feelings of what is good and right would be totally individualized. They would become little more than preferences that we might take up or throw off at no more than a whim (compare with MacIntyre's 1985 account of emotivism).

Yet these 'feelings' are worth investigating a little more. Through that investigation it will be possible to go some way towards explaining the evident paradox in the case that is developed by Bellah and his colleagues. After all they seem to be moving towards the conclusion that television serves to individualize and isolate. Yet they also seem to be wanting to argue that television promotes feelings that draw us together. If this paradox is examined it will become possible to begin to understand the close relationship between the media and compassion. Or, put another way, it will begin to become possible to answer the question, 'Why compassion?'

All of this can be achieved if the focus of attention turns towards the other text that was mentioned earlier, before the discussion of the themes that are raised by *Habits of the Heart*. That text is David Riesman's justly famous study, *The Lonely Crowd*.

Media and the other directed character

According to Riesman, and at the risk of oversimplifying a complex argument, it is possible to identify a transformation in social character in the United States. For Riesman, character can be defined as, 'the more or less permanent socially and historically conditioned organization of an individual's drives and satisfactions' and, '"Social character" is that part of "character" which is shared among significant social groups and which . . . is the product of the experience of these groups' (Riesman 1960: 4. It should be noted that Riesman consequently understands 'character' in a different way than MacIntyre. For Riesman, character is, in the first instance, a social attribute whereas for MacIntyre it is a product of virtue). By these definitions then, Riesman is saying that if attention is paid to American history, it is possible to see that the 'drives and satisfactions' of individuals have been organized differently at different moments and, moreover, that these different organizations do not reflect individual idiosyncrasies but, instead, reflect and represent the experiences of definite social groups. For Riesman, the most recent shift has been away from an 'inner directed' character and towards an 'other directed' character.

He says that the inner directed character is typical of those societies which experience expansion and rapidly increasing mobility. Riesman says that those kinds of societies (think of Britain in the nineteenth century) give individuals a huge range of choices that they have to make more or less on their own. These individuals have been uprooted from the securities and certainties of traditional societies (in which things are done in a certain way because that is the way that they have always been done), and yet they continue to need to live socially. Riesman says that in these circumstances, the dominant character type is inner directed: 'the source of direction for the individual is "inner" in the sense that it is implanted early in life by the elders and directed toward generalized but nonetheless inescapably destined goals' (Riesman 1960: 15; this sentence is emphasized in the original). So, the inner directed character is educated in the goals of the specific social and cultural milieu of which she or he is a part. Those goals become guiding principles for everything that she or he does. Indeed, insofar as those goals are successfully internalized, there can be a fairly high degree of confidence that the individuals will continue to uphold them even if no one is around to keep an eye on them. For example, it is probably the case that when he was lost in Africa, Dr Livingstone continued to shave and to wear 'decent' clothing. He was an inner directed man whose every deed and action was guided by the goals and values of the wider society which had been drummed into his head through schooling and his social and cultural context. Had he stopped shaving or trimming his moustache, Dr Livingstone would have stopped being himself.

Now, if Riesman's definition of inner direction is modified slightly, it can be used to cast some light on the issue of the competing logics of journalistic practice. The point is that although Riesman sees historical shifts in dominant social character types, there is no reason to assume that the shift is a coherent and cohesive single rupture with the past. Even when social and cultural relationships are not characterized by expansion, it is possible for character to remain inner directed. All that is needed is the possibility of education in terms of a firm set of values and principles which the individual might internalize in such a way that they become an indivisible aspect of her or his sense of self. It can be speculated that this is exactly what happens to those journalists who are trained in the goals and principles of objective practice. These journalists internalize values of practice to such an extent that to challenge them is to undermine their sense of self-worth and integrity. And yet those principles make it possible for them to go from killing field to killing field, reporting with ostensible impartiality everything that they see and hear: 'The inner-directed person becomes capable of maintaining a delicate balance between the demands upon him of his life goal and the buffetings of his external environment' (Riesman 1960: 16). In this way, it is also reasonable to link the inner directed character with the theme of virtue that has been derived from MacIntyre. The inner directed journalist is capable of virtue precisely because her or his journalistic action is guided by the 'life goal' (or to put it into MacIntyre's terms, the good) that is internal to the practice of impartiality and objectivity.

Yet the tone of Riesman's study is that these inner directed character types are increasingly out of kilter with the contemporary social and cultural world. Our current world is no longer typified by the horizon of expansion but is, instead, marked by a concern to communicate with other people. This is because, thanks in no small part to the success of expansion, 'Fewer and fewer people work on the land or in the extractive industries or even in manufacturing. Hours are short. People may have material abundance and leisure besides' (Riesman 1960: 18). Or, to put the point another way, individuals are forced into situations in which they are decreasingly required to be on their own doing that which is right and proper, and are increasingly required to deal with other people. The inner directed character does not place a high premium on accommodation of the self with others and, therefore, the inner directed individual is likely to be rather abrupt if not plainly inept in her or his dealings with them. After all, the inner directed character knows what ought to be done and feels compelled to do it; if others do not agree, then that is likely to be considered as their problem. The other directed character can never be this blasé about others.

Whereas the inner directed character is possessed of a kind of inner 'gyroscope' by means of which she or he can navigate a true and reliable course through the world (Riesman 1960: 18), 'what is common to all the other-directed people is that their contemporaries are the source of direction for the individual – either those known to him or those with whom he is indirectly acquainted, through friends and through the mass media' (Riesman 1960: 21; this sentence is emphasized in the original). This claim links the discussion of the other directed character back to Max Weber's definition of social action. If the other directed character derives all direction from others and if, following Weber, social action consists in an orientation towards others, then the other directed character is forced to participate in *social* action and compelled to avoid mere action. By extension, the other directed character is also fundamentally *moral* whereas the inner directed character is much more markedly *ethical*.

For the other directed character then, the practice of virtue, on the basis of firm ethical ideals which pay no account of circumstances, is almost wholly inconceivable. The other directed character cannot ignore others. Her or his map of the social world is oriented around self and others in everyday relationships. The inner directed character wants to do what is right and proper, and the other directed character wants to do what is nice and friendly. Ethical ideals are an obstacle to that latter quest. At best they are an irrelevance and at worst they are a problem to be overcome. Of course, the remaining inner directed characters are likely to identify this situation as nothing other than a sign of the collapse of the social itself. This is exactly how Jonathan Sacks saw things after the James Bulger murder. In an almost classic statement of how the inner directed character might look at the deeds and the world of the other directed, he wrote: 'We have given children no framework within which to learn civic virtue and responsibility' (Sacks 1995: 14). For the inner directed Sacks, the framework can be provided by education and a respect for a community which gives the individual definite guidelines and principles of action. For Sacks then, the answer to the problem is more and better inner direction. The difficulty with that solution is that it ignores the distinct likelihood that those who are to be encouraged in the virtues of inner direction are, in fact, fundamentally other directed and therefore likely to be completely incapable of understanding the full import of what Sacks has in mind.

The other directed person might well be concerned with what people think but, more importantly, she or he is likely to be overly concerned with what people *feel* and to interpret the orientation towards others in terms of the *sensation* of being with them. According to Riesman, the other directed character is concerned, 'not so much in external details as in the quality of his inner experience. That is, his great sensitivity keeps him in touch with others on many more levels than the externals of appearance and propriety' (Riesman 1960: 24). This is a conclusion which resonates with the claim of Bellah and his colleagues that television is about sensation. The other directed character is in fact much less concerned with morality than with morale; with feeling good rather than being good (Riesman 1960: 37–65). In the face of that kind of character, Sacks would almost certainly throw up his hands in despair.

Just as a connection was made between inner direction and the concern with objectivity and impartiality which constitutes one of the logics within the sphere of journalistic practice, so similarly a connection can be made between this other directed quest for sensation and the logic of sensationalism and the human interest. Journalistic practice in terms of the logic of market sensationalism tends not, of course, to derive its paramount legitimacy and validity through a reference to the 'facts' of the case. Instead, this kind of journalistic practice is legitimized and validated to the extent that it is able to communicate some sense of what it feels like either to witness such scenes of suffering and misery or, more ambitiously, what it might be like to experience them for oneself. Consequently, journalistic practice which stresses the dimension of human interest will tend to emphasize sensation, bolstered by an attempt to represent the inner feelings of the journalists and victims themselves. Sensational journalistic practice is sensational in both senses of the word.

In his account of the rise of the other directed character type (which is of course much more nuanced and subtle than the very broad overview that has been provided in this discussion), Riesman continually returns to the significance of the media. Yet he does this in a way which evidently supports the argument we have been developing that there is a difference of logics within the sphere of journalistic production and that this split is reflected to some extent in the coexistence of inner and other directed journalistic characters. In the context of a discussion of the relationship between the media and politics, Riesman comments that, 'the much criticized media – especially the press – seem to have maintained a surprisingly inner-directed attitude toward the political'. For example, Riesman points out that even tabloid newspapers tend to give front page space to political stories (even if the stories are spun through narratives of sex or dishonesty) and 'in this way they help maintain the prestige of politics as a presumed interest on the part of their audiences' (Riesman 1960: 197, 198). The question that Riesman asks is why politics continues to be given this place of importance. His answer highlights the dominance of other directed character types within media institutions: 'One reason for this is the desire of those who work for the mass media to do what is right or considered to be right by those to whom they look for leadership' (Riesman 1960: 198).

What this means, although Riesman does not draw out the point, is that the ethical ideals that the media might uphold and proclaim are subject to what amounts to two kinds of contingency. First, they are transformed from ideal goals which substantiate certain virtuous practices and into principles of the manipulation of others. This point is implicit to Riesman's contention that media professionals seek to do what is considered to be right 'by those to whom they look for leadership'. As soon as the ethical is redirected away from the ideal and towards the desires and interests of particular powerful social and cultural groups, it becomes little more than a means through which others might be encouraged to engage in practical action that is in the interests of the powerful. Ethics thereby tend to become preferences. Moreover, the powerful groups are not confined to political institutions. Given that the media operate in a commercial world, the powerful groups also include the audience itself. As such, media professionals always keep a weather-eye on the opinions and sensibilities of the audience, simply to reflect them back in a circle of mutual justification. In this way ethics becomes identical with an inner sensation of feeling good about one's world and one's self. Second, the ethical is subject to contingency because there is no reason to assume that the powerful groups will remain the same and unchanging or, indeed, that journalists are capable of any undistorted and 'correct' expression of their interests. Journalists might get it wrong, the powerful might be thrown out of office or it might be thought that the audience has changed its opinions (hence the importance of opinion polls and market research to commercial media). In either case, ethics are undermined and turned into more or less transitory or arbitrary principles of action. They occasion a certain cynicism and incredulity. And so, once again, the other directed character is forced to orient her- or himself towards the actions and expressions of others and this character can only know deep feeling through overwhelming sensation. Nothing else remains (to recall the phrase from *Habits of the Heart*).

The dimensions of compassion

Going beyond Riesman, it can be proposed that compassion plays a crucial role in the orientations and sensations of the other directed character. It can be suggested that compassion provides those orientations with a sensation of deep worth and value which can also possess a dimension of external (that is, other directed) display. But how can compassion in particular play this role?

Perhaps the most obvious answer to that question was offered in Chapter 2, when it was suggested that contemporary social actors are the heirs to a certain history of moral sensibility and consciousness in the West. That history has emphasized compassion and, therefore, compassion is a fundamental dimension of the kinds of people that we are. That answer is very neat but undoubtedly it is much too simplistic. It can never entirely overcome the difficulty of explaining how it can be that something which is historically and socially contingent can come to possess a quality of being natural and inevitable. Moreover, this initial answer cannot deal with the problem of explaining how it can be that, from an analytical point of view at least, compassion seems to remain immune to the trials and tribulations of other ethical ideals and moralities in the circumstances and conditions of incommensurability. This is indeed an important point to stress. Even though we might glimpse the difficulties that are created by incommensurability, and even though we might even begin to glimpse some of the reasons why incommensurability can lead to violence, it is nevertheless the case that compassion is never really questioned. Certainly, compassion can exacerbate ethical confusion (such that, for example, it is possible to feel moral sympathy both for the woman who is accidentally pregnant and for the foetus that is to be aborted), but the point remains that compassion itself is rarely questioned. It always *feels* right, even if it does lead us into contradiction. How can this be?

Riesman's account of the rise of the other directed character indicates the possibility of an alternative answer. Riesman would imply that compassion is so central to contemporary moral sensibilities precisely because contemporary character is overwhelmingly other directed. As Riesman would doubtless point out, rigorous ethical systems such as Kant's categorical imperative or, for that matter, any conception of virtue, require characters who are fundamentally inner directed. For example, virtue requires that individual actors consistently and continually ask themselves whether they are becoming the kind of person that the codes of virtue demand. Similarly, Kant's categorical imperative is predicated on the assumption that individual actors are able to think before they perform any given action and ask themselves whether it is possible consistently to will that the maxim of the action can be universalized (that is to say, can I want everyone else to do as I am about to do?). Both of these approaches enjoin – and for that matter defend and promote – the inner directed character. This is because they require that the individual actor is possessed of a kind of inner gyroscope which will always guide and determine action in line with ideals and goals that have been learnt and inculcated through education of one sort or another. They both require that the individual actor pays a lot more attention to assessments of what ought to be done rather than to considerations of what other people might want or desire to be done, or what it might be expedient to do in this particular situation.

Compassion is not like that at all. It does not require consistency and coherence over time and neither does it require that individual social actors engage in a turmoil of inner debate and deliberation before they do anything at all. Instead, compassion requires that individual actors orient themselves towards others and, in particular, towards what others appear to be experiencing. If those others are not seen to be experiencing suffering or misery, then compassion can remain at a latent level. It needs only to become overt and explicit, it needs only to be the basis for any deliberate action on the part of the individual social actor, as soon as those others are seen to be in situations that warrant some sense of empathy and fellow-feeling. Consequently, compassion is a moral sensibility which is in many ways tailor made for the demands and horizons of the other directed character. It emphasizes attending to others and it implies that the individual need feel no ethical or moral concerns all the time that others are not seen to be suffering or miserable. Compassion means an orientation towards others in order to work out what ought to be done, and if those others provide no clues or no incitement then it is possible to believe that nothing needs to be done.

Perhaps this speculation can be extended to explain some of the dimensions of compassion fatigue that Kinnick, Krugman and Cameron discovered in their study. It can be speculated that what they uncovered was the ethical and moral emptiness of the other directed character when the suffering of others is not noticed. Or, to put the point more strongly, without the presence of suffering others, the other directed character feels no ethical compulsions at all. Compassion is like a jack-in-the-box, waiting to spring out and create an appearance of activity but kept in the dark all the time no one opens the lid.

Yet there is a difficulty with that answer as well. If compassion is tied so tightly to the nature and the needs of the other directed character, the logic of the argument is that compassion is little more than a neat and easy solution to the problems of ethics which the other directed character confronts. After all, no one wishes to be thought by their peers to be utterly cruel and heartless, and no one wishes to be considered to be totally without any ethical and moral heart. But, as we have seen, the other directed character derives an appearance – and thereby an inner sense – of moral worth from compassion. It could well be that compassion is all there is on offer for the individual actor who would be moral in contemporary social and cultural relationships (after all, ideals, goals and codes have been undermined by incommensurability and debunking) and, moreover, it could well be that compassion is experienced by those actors as plausible, valid and appropriate. This is the issue that our analysis has got to be able to explain. This is the issue of the subjective plausibility and belief in the adequacy of a kind of moral sensibility which, from an analytical perspective, seems to be so implausible and inadequate. A very suggestive way of grappling with this issue, and of relating it to the concerns of this book, is provided if attention is paid to some of the work of Carol Gilligan.

Gilligan's work is an expansion and an exploration of the implications of an empirical observation that she made as a psychologist, looking at conventional academic accounts of the moral development of children. Gilligan noticed that when moral development is understood in terms of a scale of progress, with an ability to uphold and practically act upon abstract ideals defined as the peak of development, girls and women tend to score remarkably badly. She noticed by contrast that boys tend to get high scores when moral development is assessed by this kind of scale. If these scales of moral development are valid and accurate, the inevitable conclusion is that boys and men tend to be much more morally competent and aware than girls and women who thereby become consigned to some kind of nether world of an almost stunted moral competence.

Rather than accept this conclusion at face value, Gilligan manages to show that it reflects a certain bias in theories of moral development and that, rather than judging women as being less morally competent than men, they ought instead to be judged as expressing a different **moral voice**. Gilligan argues that boys and men score well in the conventional tests because, like the tests themselves, their understandings and interpretations of morality are organized around abstract ideals and rules. Meanwhile girls and women score less well because their moral voice is organized around relationships of care. These relationships are usually identified by the tests with a lower stage of the development of moral competence. While men tend to uphold an ethic of justice and fairness, women tend to uphold an ethic of care and responsibility: 'This conception of morality as concerned with the activity of care centers moral development around the understanding of responsibility and relationships, just as the conception of morality as fairness ties moral development to the understanding of rights and rules' (Gilligan 1993: 19).

An example of the distinction between moral voices which Gilligan seeks to make is provided by a discussion she provides of different responses to what psychologists call 'Heinz's dilemma'. The dilemma was presented by Gilligan to 11-year-old boys and girls. It was developed by the psychologist Lawrence Kohlberg in order to measure moral development, and it asks children to resolve the problem of Heinz who 'considers whether or not to steal a drug which he cannot afford to buy in order to save the life of his wife' (Gilligan 1993: 25).

Gilligan reports how Jake and Amy deal with Heinz's problem after being asked whether or not he should steal the drug. Jake decides that Heinz should steal the drug. Jake reasons on the basis that although such an action would be illegal, most people (including the judge at any trial) would recognize that Heinz was upholding a moral principle about the value of life. It would be appreciated that Heinz was not stealing the drug for his own benefit, and would not have stolen it at all if he had enough money to buy it. Jake tries to work out the problem logically and draws a distinction between morality and law. Gilligan reports that Jake tries to resolve the problem by appealing to autonomous values and ideals which stand over and above any given individual (Gilligan 1993: 27). Amy resolves the predicament in a different way. Amy decides that Heinz should not steal the drug to save his wife. But she does not reach this conclusion on the basis of the law but on the basis of an emphasis upon the need to maintain relationships. Amy reasons that, 'If he stole the drug, he might save his wife then, but if he did, he might have to go to jail, and then his wife might get sicker again . . . so, they should really just talk it out and find some other way to make the money' (quoted in Gilligan 1993: 28). Gilligan reports that whereas Jake sees the dilemma as an abstract problem, Amy sees a 'narrative of relationships that extends over time'. Contrary to Jake, who sees people standing detached from one another trying to resolve abstract issues, Amy sees 'a world comprised of relationships' and attachments (Gilligan 1993: 29).

Gilligan points out that on the conventional psychological scales of the measurement of moral competence, Jake would score considerably higher than Amy. This is because Jake stresses abstract ideals of justice and fairness whereas Amy emphasizes immediate enduring relationships of care. But, Gilligan wants to contend, that kind of hierarchical comparison and, implicitly, judgement of the judgement of others, misses the crucial point that Jake and Amy attempt to resolve the Heinz dilemma in radically different ways (see note 1).

Now, Gilligan is a good and subtle enough analyst not to reduce these different voices to innate and gender specific capacities and qualities. In work which has returned to the initial claim that the moral development of women is not worse than that of men, just different, she has also sought to move away from any tendency to over-polarize the debate and to claim that men cannot be caring and that women cannot be fair or just. Rather, Gilligan contends that the different moral voices reflect the different dramas of childhood that men and women tend to experience. The corollary of this claim is that the different voices will therefore be gender *focused* rather than gender *specific*.

In an article that Gilligan wrote with her colleague Grant Wiggins, the contention was made that, 'We locate the origins of morality in the young child's awareness of self in relation to others' (Gilligan and Wiggins 1988: 114). That awareness of self in relationship has two dimensions. First, there is the dimension of inequality, 'reflected in the child's awareness of being smaller and less capable than adults and older children, of being a baby in relation to a standard of human being'. According to Gilligan and Wiggins, this feeling of powerlessness and dependency has been the dimension of children's awareness stressed in conventional psychological testing of moral development. It leads to a definition of 'morality as justice' and it emphasizes 'progress toward a position of equality and independence' (Gilligan and Wiggins 1988: 114). Here then (and relating this claim back to the themes in Gilligan's earlier book, *In a Different Voice*; I am using the second (1993) edition of a book that was originally published in 1982), it can be contended that insofar as boys in conventional socialization experience the drama of dependence and the struggle for independence more strongly than girls (because boys are taught to detach themselves from the family background and that it is their role to participate in the impersonal world of work), their moral horizons will tend to focus on questions of the equality of autonomous actors, and therefore they will stress invariant ideals and rules of justice, fairness, moral equality and so forth (Gilligan and Wiggins 1988: 116).

However, Gilligan and Wiggins also highlight the second dimension of the child's development. They point out that, 'the young child also experiences attachment, and the dynamics of attachment relationships create a very different awareness of self – as capable of having an effect on others, as able to move others and to be moved by them'. Children are attached to those who care for them and with whom love relationships develop. Gilligan and Wiggins continue to state that, 'In the context of attachment, the child discovers the patterns of human interaction and observes the ways in which people care for and hurt one another' (Gilligan and Wiggins 1988: 114–15). This dimension of early relationships leads to a morality that stresses the importance of a responsibility to care for others and to attend to their feelings, needs and desires. And to the extent that in conventional socialization girls are taught the values of familial care and the responsibility to attend to others, their moral voices will tend to focus on questions of attachment, concern and relationship (Gilligan and Wiggins 1988: 116).

These themes can be applied to the issue of compassion and, by extension, to the question of compassion fatigue. Certainly, the issues that are raised by Carol Gilligan's work make it unfortunate, to say the least, that the Kinnick, Krugman and Cameron study gives no indication of the gender breakdown or gender focus of respondents. If Gilligan's work is valid it would not be unreasonable to expect there to be a gender divide in attitudes towards compassion fatigue. It is likely that men, insofar as their development is oriented around questions of detachment which lead to a moral voice focused around issues of justice and fairness, would experience compassion fatigue much more quickly than women and, moreover, it can be speculated that they would be much more inclined than women to hold the sufferers responsible for whatever it is that ails them. Meanwhile, it is reasonable to propose that women, insofar as their development is more marked by questions of attachment which lead to a moral voice focused around issues of care and responsibility, would be slower to experience compassion fatigue. Furthermore, women would be much more likely than men to identify compassion fatigue as a problem. If Gilligan's work is valid, women are likely to constitute a significantly more compassionate media audience than men (although, to repeat a point that was made earlier, Gilligan's work points to gender *foci* rather than gender *specificity* concerning the different moral voices and, therefore, it is not at all being suggested that no men can be compassionate or that no women can uphold abstract ideals like justice and fairness).

In these terms, it is largely besides the point whether or not men or women are more likely than the other to read or watch news. Indeed, even if studies might indicate that men are far more voracious news consumers than women, this does not invalidate the applicability of Gilligan's work. From this point of view, the *quantity* of news consumption has no necessary implications for the *quality* of that reading and watching.

Conclusion

What this intimation of different moral voices reveals is the absolute inescapability of ethical incommensurability. It would seem to be the case that contemporary social and cultural relationships are fated to be marked by the kind of 'shrillness' about which MacIntyre is so concerned. Indeed, compassion offers no resolution of the problem that it is impossible to arbitrate between competing ethical claims and narratives. This is because compassion is itself contradictory. It is not a monolith. As Gilligan and Wiggins demonstrate, the meaning of compassion is variable and dependent upon whether it is harnessed to the moral voice of justice or to the moral voice of care. Put differently, it can be suggested that compassion merely compounds the problems and exacerbates the dilemmas which are inevitably confronted by other directed character types who take their bearings from their peers and those whom they see around them. The response to the suffering and misery that is shown on the screen or reported on the page will therefore vary dependent upon from *which* peers the other directed character takes her or his bearings.

It is one thing to say that compassion is a moral sensibility which involves the individual social actor feeling the suffering and the misery of the other, but 'the suggestion of a family of feelings mediated by standards of feeling to which everyone is assumed to have access leaves open the question of how this access is gained' (Gilligan and Wiggins 1988: 122). For Gilligan and Wiggins of course, it is exactly the matter of how access is gained that cuts to the heart of the issue of the different dimensions of moral development. To this extent they draw an important distinction between co-feeling and empathy. According to Gilligan and Wiggins, 'empathy implies an identity of feelings – that self and other feel the same' (Gilligan and Wiggins 1988: 122). The presumption of empathy, then, is that the individual actor and the other are detached and separate from one another. Empathy therefore raises questions of justice and fairness and is likely to be focused more among men than women. Meanwhile, co-feeling involves the assumption that access to the feelings of others, 'develops through the experience of relationships which render *others'* feelings accessible . . . Co-feeling, then, depends on the ability to *participate* in another's feelings (in their terms), signifying an attitude of engagement rather than an attitude of judgment or observation'. Gilligan and Wiggins continue to say that, 'To feel with another any emotion means in essence to be *with* that person, rather than to stand apart and look *at* the other, feeling sympathy *for* her or him' (Gilligan and Wiggins 1988: 122).

Yet if one of the two moral voices which dominate in contemporary social and cultural relationships is indeed focused around the kind of detachment that means looking *at* the other, then it follows that those who speak with that voice, will tend to feel sympathy for those with whom they engage rather than any co-feeling for those with whom they live together. They will feel sorry for the suffering and the miserable, just so long as the suffering and miserable cannot be held to be responsible for their own hardship. But those who express the compassion of co-feeling are forced into a situation in which that co-feeling becomes entirely dependent upon the ability of journalistic production to make the suffering and miserable into fellow members of humanity with whom one can enter into relationships rather than merely transient images on the page or screen. Journalistic production has to be able to make it possible for at least one section of the audience to perform what amounts to an ontological leap. But the journalists themselves experience the kind of compassion fatigue which tells them that their reports and representations do not, and perhaps even cannot, achieve that kind of compulsion.

It is indeed unsurprising that there is frequently a gap between the intentions of journalists in the field of production and the kinds of social action that are likely to be engaged in by actors when they read, hear or watch those productions. Journalistic productions are not sent out to a homogeneous and monolithic audience which can be presumed to act in identical ways either in terms of any given report or representation or in terms of any given genre of report or representation. Simply because there might be social action and moral engagement in the context of the news from Ethiopia it does not at all follow that identical news from the Sudan will be the basis of anything approaching a similar response. This is because social actors do not approach reports and representations in terms of definite ethical systems between which it is possible rationally to arbitrate and to assess the significance of different claims upon action. Rather, they approach journalistic production in the context of the fundamental confusion over competing demands which is implied by ethical incommensurability. If it is presumed that the uncertainties and contingencies which are thereby thrown up might be avoided through appeals to compassion, then a further dimension of incommensurability simply rears its head; compassion means different things to different actors thanks to the existence of two competing (and gender focused) moral voices. Social action is not a monolith either in terms of expressions of concern or practices.

The conclusion seems to be clear. It is impossible to predict in advance whether, how or which journalistic production will be or become morally compelling. Social action is actually much too complex to allow for prediction.

Note

1 My colleague Graham Spencer has pointed out to me that many analysts might reject the applicability of the Heinz dilemma to a study of the moral compulsion of the media. This is because the Heinz dilemma is predicated upon the use of imagination and insight in a way that, it is said, the media actually deny. The point I am wanting to make is that Gilligan's work shows that the tendency towards monolithic theorizing which those denials tend to contain actually conceals more than it reveals. What I am trying to do is provide some of the resources by means of which it might be possible to develop a much more nuanced and subtle account than general denial-theories can allow. To put the point more empirically; it is clearly the case that, in the context of some reports and representations the audience does practice imagination and insight. But: which reports and representations? Why? Who in the audience? Those are the questions that any theory has to have the space to be able to begin to address.

Nevertheless, the denial theories are widespread and influential. They are also extremely attractive despite their lack of subtlety. They are worth outlining quickly. Fortunately, Noel Carroll has systematized the literature and he has reached the conclusion that it is possible to identify three hypotheses about how the media deny the possibility of imagination and insight on the part of the audience. Carroll

(1998) concentrates on television. It is also important to stress that he outlines these hypotheses in order to reject them through highlighting their logical inconsistencies.

First, there is the realism hypothesis. According to this hypothesis, television represents the world as it really is. Consequently, it is supposed that nothing can be done about all of this because this is simply the way that things are. The existing world becomes inevitable: 'This effect is particularly relevant for morality, since if it indeed obtains, then it would blinker the moral horizons of viewers. It would obstruct their recognition of alternatives to existing social arrangements' (Carroll 1998: 140). Second, Carroll outlines the escapism hypothesis. Within this hypothesis it is supposed that there is a disconnection of emotion from action and 'in so far as fantasy erodes or is likely to erode the linkage between emotion and action, and the linkage between emotion and action is essential for moral behaviour, fantasy as such . . . is ethically suspect because it tampers with the conditions for moral activity' (Carroll 1998: 143). Within this hypothesis then, the argument is not that television denies imagination but that it promotes too much of it, to such an extent that the audience escapes into the world of soap opera rather than confronts the moral problems of misery and suffering. Third, Carroll outlines the hypnotism thesis. According to this thesis, television dulls sensibility through quick editing and the like. Television tries to draw us in and keep us watching without bothering with whether we are actually engaging with what we see. Carroll sums up the hypnotism thesis when he begins with a statement about what imagination is said (within the hypothesis) to involve normally:

> The imagination is said to be an essential feature of moral thinking because it is the power to envision alternatives. Moral judgement presupposes the recognition that things could be otherwise. The rapid succession of structural articulations, like cutting, does not allow the spectator the time to imagine moral alternatives; one is so occupied in simply attending to the visual array that there is no space for the moral imagination to take root. Thus, by precluding the operation of the moral imagination with respect to fictional and documentary material that calls for moral judgement, the typical structuring of television imagery is morally suspect.
>
> (Carroll 1998: 148)

As Carroll knows, and as this book also seeks to show, the theoretical and empirical situation is much more complex than any of those hypotheses can adequately allow.

Further reading

Bellah, R.N., Madsen, R., Sullivan, W.M., Swidler, A. and Tipton, S.M. (1986) *Habits of the Heart: Individualism and Commitment in American Life*. New York: Harper and Row.

Gilligan, C. (1993) *In a Different Voice: Psychological Theory and Women's Development* (2nd edition). Cambridge, MA: Harvard University Press.

Gilligan, C. and Wiggins, G. (1988) The origins of morality in early childhood relationships, in C. Gilligan, J.V. Ward and J. McLean Taylor (eds) *Mapping the Moral Domain: A Contribution of Women's Thinking to Psychological Theory and Education*. Cambridge, MA: Harvard University Press.

Kinnick, K.N., Krugman, D.M. and Cameron, G.T. (1996) Compassion fatigue: communication and burnout toward social problems, *Journalism and Mass Communications Quarterly*, 73(3): 687–707.

Riesman, D. (1960) *The Lonely Crowd: A Study of the Changing American Character*. With N. Glazer and R. Denney. New Haven, CT: Yale University Press.

LIFTING THE LID ON COMPASSION

Introduction

Towards the end of Chapter 3, it was suggested that compassion can be understood as being a little like a jack-in-the-box. What that metaphor means is that it is wrong to interpret compassion as an always and already active way in which the social actor deals with the world. Compassion is not ever present in that manner. Rather, compassion is a kind of moral engagement that is active, and indeed felt by social actors, only as and when an appropriate and a relevant occasion arises. The logical corollary is that, as Hannah Arendt argued, once the occasion which stimulates compassion disappears, so too does the sense of outrage which the feeling involves (Arendt 1973b: 24). As such, and relating all of this to the definition of morality as social action which was provided at the beginning of Chapter 3, it can be proposed that compassion is identifiable as morality only as and when it is the basis of distinctive forms of social action on the part of the actors who together constitute the audience. All the time that compassion does not occasion action, logically it cannot be identified with morality. Instead, it is a personality trait.

Compassion is latent, waiting to spring up when the lid is raised on the emotion. That is why compassion is like a jack-in-the-box. But that contention leaves a rather important question dangling in the air. It is one thing to say that compassion is there waiting to spring up when the lid is raised, but that gives us no insight whatever into precisely what it is that does manage to raise the lid on the box. Or, to put all of this into something more like an analytical question, we need to ask: what and which media reports and representations are likely to be the causes of compassion on the part of different actors within the audience?

That is where the situation begins to get extremely complicated. A one-dimensional application of the compassion fatigue thesis would suggest that *all* reports and representations have become decreasingly capable of lifting the lid on compassion. This is because, so the argument would run, the audience has become desensitized to the news about suffering and misery. Meanwhile, those commentators who have identified the traces of compassion fatigue amongst journalists would reach a broadly similar conclusion, albeit by a different route. They would tend to say that the lid can no longer be lifted because the journalists themselves have become jaded and tired to such an extent that either they do not notice suffering and misery when it is before them or, if they do notice it, they no longer have the ability to communicate precisely how terrible it is.

But, as the preceding chapters have tried to indicate, one-dimensional and monolithic applications of the compassion fatigue thesis are lacking in analytical sophistication (notwithstanding the many and considerable logical problems of all discussions about the purported phenomenon). In Chapter 2 it was argued that compassion fatigue is best understood as a response by photographers and reporters to some of the stresses and strains that are created for them by the conflicts within the field of journalistic production. The argument was developed that it is sociologically more valid to identify the discussion about compassion fatigue as one example of the attempt by journalists who operate predominantly according to the virtues of objectivity, to explain exactly why it is that the audience fails to respond to a given report or representation in the way that was originally intended. Consequently, it was also being suggested that the moral compulsion of reports and representations is not reducible to the direct and straightforward expression of the intentions of the photographer or reporter (or, for that matter, the editor) who is the producer of the news. Rather, moral compulsion is the result of a complex interplay between the place of the report or representation in the field of journalistic production and the meanings and moral horizons which the audience brings to the media, from outside. After all, the moral horizons of the audience (and therefore the moral framework within which the report or representation is situated and implicated) are to a considerable extent independent of the media.

All of this means that the audience itself should not be understood as being entirely reducible to the media of which it is the reader, viewer or listener. Instead, it is analytically more appropriate to identify the audience as a social constituency which coalesces around and in terms of the media but which also has dimensions of subjectivity that are beyond and independent of the media themselves. It was the concern of Chapter 3 to seek to unravel some of those broader contextual factors which shape how the audience understands and interprets moral compulsion. The complexity within the audience means that it is more or less completely meaningless to make all-inclusive comments of the order that there is a general condition of compassion fatigue. That kind of statement is meaningless precisely because the audience is not a monolith. As we saw, it is logically valid to contend that the audience is possessed of compassion in two, different and gender-focused, ways. It therefore follows that even if the compassion fatigue thesis is, with all necessary caution, supposed to be applicable to one part of the audience it does not at all follow that it casts any light on another part. What we have seen is that the situation is exceedingly complex, variable and multifaceted.

But still the point remains that the lid has to be lifted on the compassion if moral action is going to ensue. Here then, the problem that emerges from the logic of the argument which has been developed so far in this book, runs parallel to an empirical fact. The social actors who together constitute the audience *do* indeed engage in moral action. They do indeed try to 'do something' about suffering and misery which is recognized only thanks to the press and broadcasting. Of course, it would be quite wrong to argue that there is anything necessary about this action. As we can see, there is nothing necessary about the action at all. Both theoretically (in terms of the argument which has been developed so far in this book) and empirically (if we attend to what actually happens in the world), it is perfectly obvious that action is engaged in only sometimes and not necessarily consistently.

So, what lifts the lid? Do different reports and representations lift the lid for the different parts of the audience? Is there some kind of privileged report or representation that can be relied upon always to stir up the compassion of everyone who sees it? (After all, most moral action tends to be carried out by men *and* women, although that is not to say that they act for identical reasons or because of identical interpretations of what is going on.) Or are the meanings and implications of reports and representations marked by the condition of moral incommensurability? Do other factors surrounding journalistic production have an impact upon the likelihood of any given report or representation inspiring the compassion of anyone (let alone everyone)? These are some of the questions that this chapter seeks to explore.

Guilt and love

The work of Carol Gilligan and her colleagues provides a basis upon which it is possible to offer some theoretical claims about how the lid might be lifted on compassion. As we have seen, Gilligan claims that it is possible to identify two different, gender-focused, 'moral voices'. First, there is a moral voice which upholds notions of justice that is gender-focused amongst men and, second, there is the moral voice of care which is gender-focused amongst women. Gilligan has provided a nice summary of these voices in an article produced with her colleague Jane Attanucci. They write that, 'A justice perspective draws attention to problems of inequality and oppression and holds up an ideal of reciprocity and equal respect'. Meanwhile, 'A care perspective draws attention to problems of detachment or abandonment and holds up an ideal of attention and response to need'. Gilligan and Attanucci say that, 'Two moral injunctions – not to treat others unfairly and not to turn away from someone in need – capture these different concerns' (Gilligan and Attanucci 1988: 73).

Gilligan and Attanucci show that these moral perspectives derive from experiences in childhood development and that they reflect problems and issues in relationships for all children. They are not claiming that men are uncaring or that women are unconcerned with justice. Rather what Gilligan and her colleagues consistently and rigorously demonstrate is that, 'concerns about justice and care are both represented in people's thinking about moral dilemmas, but people tend to focus on one set of concerns and minimally represent the other'. Indeed, 'there is an association between moral orientation and gender such that both men and women use both orientations, but Care Focus dilemmas are more likely to be presented by women and Justice Focus dilemmas by men' (Gilligan and Attanucci 1988: 82). One of the important implications of this discovery is that it therefore follows that moral feelings will be felt differently dependent upon whether the social actor's moral orientations are primarily justice or care focused. Those different foci mean that the sense of moral outrage that social actors can feel will itself take different forms and be open to different interpretations and meanings.

This time with Grant Wiggins, Gilligan develops the point that each moral voice will feel moral outrage differently. The moral voice of justice will tend to feel outrage through senses of shame and guilt (Gilligan and Wiggins 1988: 120). The actor feels a sense of shame that injustice is perpetrated in the world and guilt that she, or in Gilligan's terms more probably he, is merely a spectator upon the suffering and misery of others. It is not unreasonable to propose that the feeling of guilt will be attenuated quite considerably when outrage is stimulated by the media. After all, in the contemporary West, media use tends to take place either in leisure time or in the domestic sphere (which, however deprived that domestic sphere might be, is likely to be identified by the actor with a certain semblance of minimal safety and comfort yet which is also typified by a gendered division of labour). There is an imbalance in the material relationship between the audience which reads the newspaper or watches the television and the suffering and miserable other on the page or the screen. The audience is in a position of relative leisure and safety while the suffering other is in a position of frequently absolute destitution. Now, if guilt is, as Gilligan and Wiggins (1988) reasonably suggest, stimulated by a sense of injustice then, in these terms, the injustice is likely to be felt all the more pressingly thanks to the media. In the relationship between the audience and the suffering other the imbalance is so profound that a sense of injustice will be exacerbated to an almost terminal degree. Shame and guilt will become all the stronger because the audience is so detached from the other that the feeling that 'something has to be done' cannot translate into the imagination and the practice that 'I can do it'.

Indeed, Gilligan and Wiggins make it clear that imbalances and inequalities, which are comparable to those which are implied by the relationship between the audience and the suffering other, are at the very heart of the moral emotions of shame and guilt. They write that, 'The moral emotions of shame and guilt convey a distance between self and other; to feel ashamed in the eyes of others or guilty for one's wishes or actions toward others is to feel lower than them or perhaps more powerful in the sense of being capable of doing them harm' (Gilligan and Wiggins 1988: 123). Once again, it is possible to propose that there is a clear and strong affinity between the sense of outrage that is associated with the moral voice of justice and the nature of the relationship between the media audience and the suffering other. After all, there is a profound distance between the audience and the other. That distance might not be geographical (for example, from where I am sitting writing this Kosovar refugees are much closer to me than a couple of the places I am presently planning to go to on holiday next year) but it is most certainly moral and imaginative.

The distance is an inevitable product of the fact that, despite what some of the protagonists of talk about 'time-space compression' might want to imply, there *is* a gulf between the members of the audience and the other on the screen that can never be entirely overcome. This is because, at a purely intuitive level, I watch the television or read the newspapers as an embodied being, situated in a definite and more or less solid set of social and cultural relationships which confirm my identity. I am present in the world. Meanwhile, the other on the screen has a wholly different status. She or he is flattened out in the report or representation, deprived of a definite embodied existence. Moreover, from the point of view of the audience, the suffering other is lifted out of the social and cultural context that might lend them a certain solidity. This is indeed a central component of their misery. For example, coverage of refugees invariably presents them as isolated individuals. At best, the relationships which help to confirm identity are reduced to that between the partner-less parent and his or her child. All of this is in addition to the fact that she or he is not in front of the audience for terribly long and, indeed, to the fact that it might well be that the audience only becomes aware of the suffering of this particular individual or community *after* they have already died. The other is, in a profound sense, not present in the world. It is this inequality that is undoubtedly one of the bases of the common response to reports and representations of suffering and misery that 'there is nothing I can do' or, more plaintively, 'what can I do?'

To this extent it can be contended that imbalance and inequality is the very essence of the relationship between the audience and the suffering other. In this way, it is possible for the audience to feel ashamed about the imbalance or to feel guilty that either nothing can be done to stop the suffering or, more personally, that I have done nothing about the misery. The outrage of guilt might also be a barely hidden reflection of a certain sense of unease that the audience has so much while the suffering others have so little. The inequality undermines the possibility of any action towards the other and, therefore, it tends to lead to the audience considering its own failings and failures. The audience becomes a disappointment to itself, from the perspective of its own commitments to universal moral narratives: 'When one feels ashamed or guilty in one's own eyes, the implication of inequality remains but is structured in terms of self-regard. One has fallen beneath one's standards or failed to live up to one's aspirations' (Gilligan and Wiggins 1988: 123). And self-regard means not regarding the other.

However, and bringing us back to consider the moral voice of care, Gilligan and Wiggins suggest that, 'Moral outrage can be provoked not only by oppression and injustice but also by abandonment or loss of attachment or the failure of others to respond' (Gilligan and Wiggins 1988: 120). They associate this sense of outrage with love and sorrow. However, when they use the word 'love', Gilligan and Wiggins mean it in a definite way. They are not talking about romantic love and neither are they referring to a mystical love in which the individual who feels the emotion experiences a kind of transcendence in which she or he seems to be swamped by the other: 'Instead, love is tied to the activities of relationship and premised, like attachment, on the responsiveness of human connection, the ability of people to engage with one another in such a way that the needs and feelings of the other come to be experienced and taken on as *part of* the self' (Gilligan and Wiggins 1988: 120). The partner of love is, therefore, sorrow. Sorrow is the sense of outrage that emerges within the care focus in those circumstances in which 'people' (to use the category employed by Gilligan and Wiggins) cannot engage with one another and cannot take the needs and feelings of the other into the self. Sorrow is the feeling of an unbridgeable distance.

According to Gilligan and Wiggins, the kind of moral outrage that is expressed in feelings of love and sorrow in relationship to and with the other is radically different from the shame and guilt of the moral voice of justice. Whereas shame and guilt imply a certain inequality and therefore a feeling *for* the other, love and sorrow imply the connection of feeling *with* the other. Consequently, 'the reason love does not connote condescension is not because it implies inequality but because it signifies connection. Through co-feeling, self and other, whether equal or unequal, become connected or interdependent' (Gilligan and Wiggins 1988: 123). In other words, love and sorrow are feelings which are predicated upon, and which promote, a commitment to attachments between self and others.

In this context, the relationship between the audience and the suffering and miserable other can be interpreted in a different, though not incompatible way, than it was discussed in the context of the distances and detachment that are the basis of justice concerns. It can be proposed that precisely because there is a distance between the audience and the others, the sense of moral outrage which takes the form of love and sorrow is stimulated. Whereas shame and guilt interpret distance in terms of inequality, love and sorrow construct distance as something to be overcome in the name and service of attachment. From the point of view of love and sorrow, distance does not at all lead to intimations of inequality and imbalance. Rather, it implies a need to construct relationships and a refusal to accept their lack and absence. As Gilligan and Wiggins write:

> No longer does moral inquiry turn on the question of how to live with inequality – that is, how to act *as if* self and other were, in fact, equal or how to impose a rule of equality based on a principle of equal respect. Instead, moral inquiry deals with questions of relationship pertaining to problems of inclusion and exclusion – how to live in connection with oneself and with others, how to avoid detachment or resist the temptation to turn away from need.
>
> (Gilligan and Wiggins 1988: 123)

Insofar as there is indeed and necessarily a distance between the audience and the others, it follows that those actors whose moral horizons are shaped by the care focus will tend to feel outrage as soon as they encounter reports and representations of suffering and misery. Such coverage will be interpreted as a demand not to turn away from need. For those members of the audience, such reports and representations will not be interpreted primarily as communications of affronts to justice and to the equal rights of all humans. Rather, they will tend to be interpreted as calls for attachment and to the forging of connections. From the point of view of the care focus then, outrage will tend to take the form of condemnations of the exclusion of the suffering and the miserable from either the universal moral community of humanity or from the spheres of relative safety and prosperity. There will be an emphasis upon inclusion and inclusiveness and the provision of the resources which will overcome need. Furthermore, the relevant members of the audience will condemn those who turn away from the needs of others, just as they will likely condemn themselves for refusing to see and read everything that is available, and protest against governmental and non-governmental agencies when they make it impossible to know about the suffering and the misery.

These points make it possible to reach some conclusions about the kinds of reports and representations that are most likely to be able to lift the lid on compassion. What any given report or representation has to be able to do is touch upon the different bases of moral outrage which can be found within the moral voices of justice and care. These theoretical points logically lead to two propositions. First, arguments about justice and injustice will be stimulated by those reports and representations which cause those members of the audience whose moral orientations are justice focused to feel shame and guilt. An example of such a journalistic production might be a television report about how aid agencies are unable to relieve a famine due to a lack of supplies. Here, there is no attempt to overcome distances and to connect that which is detached. Rather the primary concern is to apply universal rules of fairness. Second, arguments about care and concern will be stimulated by those reports and representations which cause those members of the audience whose moral orientations are care focused to feel love and sorrow. An example of this kind of journalistic production might be a television report about how field hospitals are having to turn away starving children or how orphanages are overflowing because the parents of children have gone missing in a wave of ethnic cleansing. Here, there is indeed a concern to overcome distance, to try to construct a kind of attachment; questions of justice (for example, questions which force me to consider whether or why the children in Kosovo make a greater claim upon me than the children in Rwanda) are entirely secondary.

But, it might be objected, these claims about morally compelling journalistic productions are derived from the logical extension of theoretical points. Is there any empirically focused literature which casts insight on what kind of report or representation stimulates compassion? The answer to that question rather seems to point to the suggestion that there is, in fact, a kind of representation which manages to touch the bases of both the justice and the care focused moral voices. Whether the bases are touched in the same way is a very different matter.

Pictures of children

Advertisers have known for quite a long time that pictures of children can be especially effective in securing the attention of an audience (Kinsey 1987). In an interesting study which was carried out with the cooperation of the charity World Vision Canada, Evelyne J. Dyck and Gary Coldevin sought to investigate whether the same held true in charitable appeals. Despite the specific focus of their study, Dyck and Coldevin (1992) raise themes and debates which help to cast light on our concerns.

Dyck and Coldevin locate their study in the context of concerns about the use of photographs by charities in their fundraising appeals. They point to the contradiction that although it could be expected that pictures which cause pleasurable feelings are likely to lead to the audience having a positive attitude towards an appeal or issue (and therefore to being well disposed towards making a financial donation), fundraisers tend to rely on pictures which are likely to cause displeasure and negative feelings in order to communicate some sense of the horrors which the appeal hopes to help alleviate. In a rather jargon laden sentence, Dyck and Coldevin write that, 'The generally supported conclusion that positive emotions lead to approach tendencies and negative emotions lead to avoidance tendencies might imply that pictures depicting people as well-fed because of donations would better evoke desired donor response than would the "starving baby appeal"'. Approach tendencies can be identified with giving money and wanting to know more, while avoidance tendencies involve turning away from this need. Yet they go on to note that, 'it is the latter that has more often been used in relief efforts, its apparent effectiveness perhaps related to evidence that among donors' main motives for giving, are guilt (for being healthy) and fear (of the disadvantaged)'. However, Dyck and Coldevin also point out that there is a widespread assumption that these images have become so ordinary and commonplace that potential donors have become largely 'desensitized' towards them (Dyck and Coldevin 1992: 573). Dyck and Coldevin's paper can be read as an enquiry into the compassion fatigue hypothesis in the specific context of fundraising for the Third World.

In their study, Dyck and Coldevin worked with World Vision Canada to develop a mail shot which used close-up photographs of African children making eye contact with the camera (and therefore, by extension, with the reader). African children were chosen for the simple reason that most of the countries named in the mail shot were in that continent. The appeal was sent to 45,855 English-speaking Canadians who had made donations to the charity during the previous year. That population was divided into three groups. One group received literature which included a positive picture of a smiling, slightly chubby child, and one group was sent the appeal this time with a photograph of an emaciated and tearful child. The third group was sent the appeal with no picture at all. Dyck and Coldevin wanted to test the hypotheses that, first, those groups which received an appeal with a photograph were more likely to make a donation – and a larger donation – than the group which received the appeal with no picture and, second, that those who received the positive photograph (of the smiling child) would be more likely to respond and yield larger average donations than those who were sent the negative picture (of the emaciated child).

What did Dyck and Coldevin discover? Not entirely what they expected. First, they found that, 'Contrary to what was predicted, the no picture donor group yielded the highest response rate and an average financial contribution larger than that of the negative photograph group'. They concluded that this finding 'would suggest that photographs did not seem to play as important a role as was anticipated'. Evidence from questionnaires suggested to Dyck and Coldevin that many potential donors thought that pictures of children would have no influence upon them and that, in any case, the money spent on the photograph would be better spent helping the child (Dyck and Coldevin 1992: 576). However, the second finding was rather more along the lines of what was hypothesized at the outset. The research showed that, 'Response rate and average financial contribution of the positive photograph group [of the smiling, slightly chubby child] were both, as predicted, higher than those of the negative photograph [of the emaciated, unhappy child] group' (Dyck and Coldevin 1992: 576). What these findings were taken to demonstrate was that while photographs did not play as much of a role in eliciting financial donations as was expected, it was nevertheless clearly the case that, 'a positive photograph had a significantly more favorable effect on donor response (both in quantitative and practical terms) than did a negative photograph' (Dyck and Coldevin 1992: 577).

When they seek to explain why the no photograph group gave the highest average donation, Dyck and Coldevin argue that this is because potential donors like to feel that they are giving money according to good, rational reasons and not on account of any tug of the heart-strings (even though other research demonstrates that actually money is donated for exactly opposite reasons. It would seem that there is a gap between what we do and why we like to think that we do it: Lewis 1983). As Dyck and Coldevin write: 'Even though emotion outsells intellect in a fund-raising context, people like to think that they are actually donating money for logical reasons'. They speculate that texts are commonly associated with rationality, pictures with emotion and that, therefore, the all-text mail shot will be identified by its recipients as making a logical argument rather than an emotive one (Dyck and Coldevin 1992: 577).

The second finding that Dyck and Coldevin need to explain is that the positive photograph group made a higher average donation than the negative photograph group. They speculate that this is because the positive photograph made potential donors feel that the appeal was likely to have a tangible beneficial effect, whereas the negative photograph rather more tended to make its recipients feel that there was nothing to be done about the enormity of suffering in Africa. According to Dyck and Coldevin, this explains why the positive photograph group made a larger average donation. The members of that group were more likely to feel that their donation would add to the success of the fieldwork of the charity.

However, within the responses to the photographs, there was a further anomaly which Dyck and Coldevin had to try to explain. This was the fact that, notwithstanding the difference in average donation, the response rate of the positive and negative photograph groups was more or less the same. There was no discernible variation between approach and avoidance tendencies. In substantive terms this means that whilst I would be more likely to make a larger donation than you if I received the picture of the smiling child and you received the one of the emaciated child, we are as likely as each other actually to make a donation. Dyck and Coldevin speculate that this anomaly is 'perhaps due to desensitization, which would have a stabilizing effect on response rates of the negative group' (Dyck and Coldevin 1992: 578). This conclusion returns the debate to the compassion fatigue hypothesis. The latent claim is that the members of the one group are as likely as the members of the other to make a donation because, notwithstanding other variables, all members of the audience have been similarly worn down by the relentlessness of the news of suffering and misery. 'Desensitization' has allegedly flattened out the variations of approach and avoidance. In the end Dyck and Coldevin resort to a fairly flat version of the compassion fatigue hypothesis and, to a considerable extent, they simply argue within it.

But it should be clear from points which have already been made in the course of this book that compassion is not as simple as Dyck and Coldevin imply. In particular, the work of Gilligan and her colleagues strongly implies that it is inappropriate and unsustainable to hold to a one-dimensional version of the compassion fatigue thesis, which would imply that all actors are similarly worn down on account of the fact that they are all members of the same audience. As Gilligan's work shows, it is important to attend to the different, and fundamentally gender-focused (although to repeat once again, emphatically not gender specific) meanings of compassion. This is a variable which Dyck and Coldevin's study ignores. It is noticeable, and undoubtedly significant for their conclusions, that their study pays no attention to the gender of the respondents. They are unable to cast any light on the possibility that each response to the mail shot was itself gender-focused. However, if Gilligan's insights are applied to the findings of Dyck and Coldevin's study it is possible, with all due caution and care, to make a number of speculations about the possible gender focus of each response.

First, in the context of Gilligan's work, it seems likely that the donors from Dyck and Coldevin's no photograph group were predominantly men. As we have seen, the donors from this group tended to respond on the basis of a belief that the appeal had constructed a rational and logically compelling case which demanded some kind of recognition and action. The case was given this sense of legitimacy precisely because the respondents felt that the appeal was *not* being made on emotional grounds. From this it logically follows that the no photograph donors must have felt that a rational argument was being made about the need for all people to be treated fairly and equally irrespective of their social and cultural attributes. The case was being made on the basis of claims and contentions about what is *just*. If the case was rationally compelling, it could not be expressing the moral voice of care, and it had to be expressing the moral orientation of justice. Consequently, the lack of a photograph would tend to be identified as unproblematic by men or, to put the case more strongly, the presence of a photograph (of whatever kind, positive or negative) might well tend to be identified as a problem by men because it would be replacing an argument about justice with an argument about emotional attachments.

Second, and carrying through with this application of themes from Gilligan, it can be suggested that the photographs would be effective spurs to a donation from women. This is because they would have raised questions about attachment and the need for care. Such feelings would have been attenuated by the fact that the photographs were closely cropped so that they showed a child, on their own and out of any context other than that which was implied by their bodily condition, and making direct eye contact with the camera. The photograph – whether positive or negative – would have been understood within the moral orientation of care as being the basis of a demand for the establishment of a kind of relationship. Quite simply (and perhaps oversimplistically), it can be suggested that the positive photograph would have resonated well with the moral orientation of care because it would have lifted the lid on compassion through its stimulation of love. Meanwhile the negative photograph would have stimulated feelings of sorrow. Finally, the no photograph mail shot would probably have been less appealing for the actors of the moral orientation of care because it would have been predicated upon, and have exacerbated, relationships and feelings of detachment. The intimation that the significance and consequences of the problem can be communicated entirely through words would have served to imply that there is no human relationship between the recipient of the appeal and its ostensible subject. Indeed, the detachment would be so great that any kind of attachment would possibly become unimaginable. For the moral orientation of justice, this is not a problem (in fact it might well be a positive advantage), but for the moral orientation of care the lack of a photograph is likely to be enormously important. Yet this is not to say that the photographs would be entirely ignored from within the moral orientation of justice concerns. They would not. The photographs would have played a part in the decision of the recipient to make a donation if it managed to stimulate feelings of shame and guilt.

It is unfortunate that Dyck and Coldevin did not identify gender as a possible factor in variations of response and donation. From a theoretical point of view at least, gender can be identified as a factor of potentially enormous significance and influence.

There is a further problem with Dyck and Coldevin's study. This is the difficulty that they pay inadequate attention to the broad social and cultural context in which their potential donors are situated and, indeed, within which their photographs are examined. Of course, they refer to contextual considerations such as compassion fatigue and wider debates about marketing and fundraising strategies. However, when all is said and done, the logic of Dyck and Coldevin's study is that reports and representations of suffering and misery can be sufficiently analysed as nothing more than external stimuli to action on the part of the individual member of the audience (and that audience is reduced to a pool of donors. In these terms, the central marketing problem is one of finding the most efficient means of making individuals feel that it is more appropriate to make a donation than to not so give). That is why their study concentrates on what potential donors do after they have received a mail shot. The donors are seen as inactive until they are stimulated from outside, and the research strategy therefore becomes one of providing the stimulation and of looking at what reactions it causes.

Universalism and myth

It is necessary to move beyond the relatively confined horizons of Dyck and Coldevin's study. In particular, attention has to be paid to the fact that when the members of the audience are confronted with a photograph, they do not read it as if it were the first time they had seen such a picture. There is a history of the reading of such images and, furthermore, a series of conventions which establishes what such photographs might mean to the audience. We do not confront reports and representations innocently, without carrying a baggage which creates what amount to preconceptions about meaning, and the possibilities of meaningfulness. Not least, photographs of suffering and misery are always implicated in the history of the narrative of moral universalism. Yet the idea of moral universalism has collapsed into incommensurability. Representations in particular – but media reports as well insofar as they express and uphold an ideal of moral universalism – serve to undermine the very ethical principle which they otherwise seek to uphold.

This difficulty has been nicely uncovered by Roland Barthes, in an essay on 'The Great Family of Man' in the *Mythologies* collection (Barthes 1972). Of course, I am reading Barthes' essay in the terms of the concerns of this book. I am framing his argument differently from the way he frames it himself. It also has to be appreciated that Barthes' essay was written in the context of a special event (a photographic exhibition in Paris) and, therefore, his claims have to be expanded in order to become applicable to the question of the moral compulsion of the media. But, remarkably, if we think about media reports and representations of, say, famine in Africa, Barthes' essay casts immediate and interesting light.

The exhibition about which Barthes wrote consisted of a series of photographs which sought to show that human actions tend to be common despite the differences of ethnicity or nationality. The exhibition suggested that despite everything, for humans there is always birth, death, knowledge and play. The exhibition sought to show that, 'there is a family of Man' (Barthes 1972: 100). By extension, it can be proposed that the exhibition was attempting to make it possible to visualize the idea of moral universalism. In and of themselves, taken on their own, the photographs might not have possessed any great moral quality. But they came to possess that extra dimension of meaning as soon as they were put together and, moreover, as soon as they were put together in a way which sought to show that we all have some things in common, that there is a kind of universality about being human. Barthes highlighted how the Paris exhibition sought to depict a 'myth of the human "community", which serves as an alibi to a large part of our humanism' (Barthes 1972: 100).

According to Barthes, this '**myth**' has two strands. It works in two ways. First, 'the difference between human morphologies is asserted, exoticism is insistently stressed, the infinite variations of the species, the diversity of skins, skulls and customs are made manifest' (Barthes 1972: 100). It is relatively easy to think of examples of this kind of 'exoticization' from the world of media reports and representations about famine. The use of close-cropped photographs of lone individuals tends to draw attention to their physical attributes. Moreover, in a morally rather questionable manner, the fact that famine victims are, by definition, emaciated, draws attention not only to their bodies (and to the bones underneath the skin) but also to the variety of human bodies since the individual looking at the representation is scarcely likely to have a body which looks quite so famished. In this way, there is an intimation of diversity.

Yet, Barthes says, second, 'from this pluralism, a type of unity is magically produced: man is born, works, laughs and dies everywhere in the same way' (Barthes 1972: 100). Here it is perhaps worth thinking about the common television image of the wrapped up corpse being placed with more or less gentleness into a freshly dug grave at the feeding centre. Of course, at their most obvious level these representations are showing that the help that is being given is barely a drop in the ocean of suffering. But, in the light of Barthes' comment it can be suggested that the representations mean something more than that. The point is that even though we (that is, the social actors who together constitute the media audience in the affluent West) tend not to die of malnutrition and in complete destitution, we too perform certain rituals around the body of the dead person. Just like the sufferers on the screen, we dig fresh graves, we wrap up the body, we cry or pray at the graveside.

Similarly, it is worth thinking in this context about the images which have tended to become something of a staple on television fundraising appeals; the images of formerly famished children in a classroom and, subsequently, playing football or running around on some patch of dusty ground. The children are always shown playing happily together. Now, in the terms of the study by Dyck and Coldevin, these representations are used in the appeals because they are particularly effective stimuli of potential donors. They are effective on two obvious counts: the representations emphasize children, and the children are smiling. Yet Barthes' comments throw up the distinct possibility that there is another layer of meaning. This layer is one about the moral universality of humanity. We have all gone to school, we have all played with our school friends. The message is that we are all alike: 'and if there still remains in these actions some ethnic peculiarity, at least one hints that there is underlying each one an identical "nature", that their diversity is only formal and does not belie the existence of a common mould' (Barthes 1972: 100).

All of this makes it seem as if it is possible to use Barthes to make the point that media reports and representations of suffering and misery therefore carry a huge baggage of meaning and that they at once illustrate and justify the claims of moral universalism. To this extent the conclusion seems to be that reports and representations are part of a definite moral narrative and that the narrative is itself one of the means by which the lid might be lifted on the compassion of the audience. The reports and representations tell a story about the universality of humanity, and about the moral relevance of all humans irrespective of the local wrapping which is put on the fact of life.

But Barthes goes on to make it possible to argue that the situation might not be this clear. The point is that if a commitment to moral universalism is going to be the spur to any kind of moral action by the audience, then there also has to be a recognition on the part of the audience that the suffering and misery experienced by others is resolvable. In other words, the audience has to be able to appreciate that the suffering and misery is not inevitable, that it is an outrage to the principles of moral universalism (whether interpreted through the prism of care or justice concerns) and that action can transform the dreadful condition of the others into something more accommodating of what is taken to be adequate to the demands of human dignity. If Barthes is right this is exactly what does *not* happen.

Why not? Barthes' discussion of the Paris exhibition directly connects with, and illustrates, his formal definition of myth: 'it transforms history into nature' (Barthes 1972: 129). According to Barthes, with its stress on the human community, the exhibition 'aims to suppress the determining weight of History: we are held back at the surface of an identity, prevented precisely by sentimentality from penetrating into this ulterior zone of human behaviour' (Barthes 1972: 100). Barthes is proposing that the representation of a 'family of man' implies that our differences are unimportant and coincidental to what it is that we all share in common. Barthes writes that, 'This myth of the human "condition" rests on a very old mystification, which always consists in placing Nature at the bottom of History'. He goes on: 'Any classic humanism postulates that in scratching the history of men a little, the relativity of their institutions or the superficial diversity of their skins . . . one very quickly reaches the solid rock of a universal human nature' (Barthes 1972: 101).

Consequently, if history has meant that some people are more likely to suffer pain and misery than others then this becomes either the way that things are or, perhaps more insidiously, one more example of the diverse tapestry that is the life of humanity. In both cases, however, that which is historical is made natural; history is transformed into nature. And about nature there is little or nothing we can do. After all, as Barthes says mockingly: 'Birth, death? Yes, these are facts of nature, universal facts. But if one removes History from them, there is nothing more to be said about them:

any comment about them becomes purely tautological' (Barthes 1972: 101). Any action which is intended to resolve suffering or offer a restitution to the miserable thus becomes pointless because it means flying in the face of what is evidently inevitable.

Barthes' comments on how myth turns the social and cultural into the natural have been taken up and brought to bear on the problem of the representation of suffering by John Taylor. His book, *Body Horror* (Taylor 1998), is an intriguing, although ultimately insufficiently sociological, study of how photojournalism represents suffering and misery and, moreover, an attempt to unravel the moral implications of that coverage.

According to Taylor, it is possible to identify the tendency of stories from Africa to concentrate on the plight of refugees as a moment of the naturalization of that which is, in fact, social. He says that if we examine reports and representations from Africa, then it is invariably the case that, as well as refugees, 'other natural or so-called "native" African products include disease, misery and atrocity. Refugees are lumped together with these other "native" products and all are presented as natural, endemic and unfathomable'. The point is of course that in many cases the reasons why there are refugees or misery are not at all unfathomable: 'This treatment of refugees (as well as the other products) may overlook the way they are produced by international wars, fed by the international arms trade, or serve other forces'. Those 'other forces' include 'the Western need to perceive relative order in liberal democracies and chaos everywhere else' (Taylor 1998: 136).

Taylor develops the theme of naturalization by examining conventions of reporting and representation. He analyses a photograph which was published in the *Observer* on 24 July 1994 of a couple of Rwandans who had fled the genocide at home and found themselves in the awful refugee camps around Goma. The picture shows a woman trying to comfort a man who is in the last throes of dying from cholera. The man is looking straight at the camera (just like the children in the mail shots in the Dyck and Coldevin study). Taylor says that the report which accompanied the photograph was 'conventional in overseas stories in representing the extreme wretchedness of the scene'. The photograph is also fairly conventional in that it refers, 'in Western eyes, to the Pieta and imagery of sorrow and loss. This means that the picture, once again conventionally, appeals to individual emotional response and not to a fundamental structure of injustice that lies beyond the frame' (Taylor 1998: 136–7). It is worth noting how Taylor conflates 'imagery of sorrow and loss' with a focus on the 'structures of injustice'. In Gilligan's terms the conflation represents a mixture of justice and care orientations. To this extent, Taylor is illustrating Barthes' analysis, the only difference being that where Barthes talks about 'myth', Taylor talks about 'convention'.

But Taylor performs a move which Barthes did not. Taylor realizes that even if it is true to say that the photograph of the dying man and the caring woman is extremely conventional, and even if it is true to say that the photograph denies the importance of the social and historical factors which led to the man ending up suffering from cholera in a refugee camp, it is nevertheless the case that the photograph makes a fundamentally moral demand upon the audience. That demand is focused in the eyes of the man, looking directly at the camera (and so, once again, the discussion recalls the pictures of children in the Dyck and Coldevin study). Taylor says that even though 'the story uses devices which are familiar in all reporting' the dead hand of convention is reinvigorated morally because in the photograph, 'the dying man appears to look at the camera, and so for once viewers are invited to look death in the eye. This meeting of eyes is a direct appeal to the individual onlooker'. Taylor continues to claim that, 'Eye contact threatens to overpower the aesthetic and other conventional forms of representing foreigners, which usually allow viewers to adopt a conditional response to matters which they may feel do not concern them' (Taylor 1998: 137). The representation of the dead and dying, so long as they look directly at the camera and therefore establish some direct eye contact with the audience, can overcome convention and thus make the viewer feel that something must be done. The right picture can smash through any semblance of compassion fatigue. The right picture can inspire moral action on the part of the audience.

This leads Taylor to the conclusion that, 'the fact that photojournalism confirms Western beliefs about the brutality of these foreign worlds does not mean that viewers are bound to be numbed by the suffering of others'. Instead, 'The media – notably the broadcast media, with the press following on – can appeal on behalf of refugees or victims of famine, and bring forward practical responses . . . [T]hough suffering is represented and always belongs to someone else distant in time and place, it may work on the imagination or sensibility of viewers until it cannot be ignored' (Taylor 1998: 138). Or, put differently, the myth might be a lie, but it might also help to save lives.

Taylor recalls some themes that emerged in the Kinnick, Krugman and Cameron (1996) study of compassion fatigue. They found that compassion fatigue can be justified (in the minds of the potential moral actors of the audience) by the belief that the victims are in some way responsible for their plight. Now, there is no evidence that Taylor is aware of the Kinnick *et al.* study (it is not cited in the bibliography to his book), but he makes a similar point when he writes that, 'Whether or not people believe it is worth while helping others may depend on how they perceive physical suffering.

They may consider that the agony of others stems from their own moral and intellectual degradation'. Taylor continues to speculate that this kind of belief is not entirely absent from the rhetoric of humanitarian aid which, he says, 'to some degree requires the constant reproduction of abject images both as a justification for intervention and as the necessary restatement of a basic difference between donors and recipients'. Taylor contends that the implied difference involves, 'the belief that there is a necessary gulf between those who are civilised enough to have aid to distribute and those who are merely civilised enough to receive it' (Taylor 1998: 136). The reason why this point is worth citing and indeed developing is that, according to some media analysts, there have emerged conventions of reporting which consolidate that kind of divide and which, indeed, make humanitarian aid into a kind of 'morality play' with its own logic of the natural and inevitable.

Conventions of the morality play

The possibility that reports and representations of humanitarian crises can be interpreted in terms of conventions of a morality play has been made and explored by John C. Hammock and Joel R. Charny. According to Hammock and Charny (1996), humanitarian crises (such as famines or wars) tend to be reported according to conventions (which, to reintroduce Barthes' terms, serve to impose a naturalistic frame upon the social and historical and thereby transform it into a myth). They concentrate on television and catalogue the images which are, indeed, all too familiar: the foreign correspondent standing facing the camera 'with teeming masses of suffering Africans or Asians in the background', the Irish nurse guiding the tour of the hospital wards, the lifeless children staring at the camera and the threatening local soldiers carrying frightening weaponry in a thoroughly cavalier fashion (Hammock and Charny 1996: 115).

'These images are at once backdrop and centerpiece of what has become over the years a scripted morality play' (Hammock and Charny 1996: 115). The script determines that the crisis 'arrives with the suddenness and power of an earthquake' (note the naturalistic referents for what are often social and historical events; this is exactly what Barthes was talking about when he defined myth). After the disaster has struck, the play shows the arrival of international aid agencies such as the Red Cross, the efforts of private relief agencies in the West and, finally, the slow cranking into operation of the Western militaries (usually wearing the hats of the United Nations). Like all plays, this one has its heroes and villains. The heroes are the Western agencies and individuals who struggle against enormous obstacles, and sometimes in the face of considerable danger, to deliver the aid where it is most needed. Moreover, there is always a local angle to the relief effort. It is a staple of local television news to tell us that, 'one day Johnny was hauling cement just down the road, and the next day he was on a plane to some dangerous place to bring relief to the suffering on the other side of the globe' (Hammock and Charny 1996: 115–16). The villains are the United Nations bureaucrats who failed to mobilize in time or who failed to resist the demands of the local war lords. The cast of villains also includes the local military authorities: 'they create the emergency in the first place, harass relief agency personnel, and make the correspondents' tasks that much harder'. At first the morality play does not have a happy ending. It usually reaches a peak with reports of riots in the feeding centres or food rotting in the distribution depots, but soon the relief agencies manage to get the situation under control and slowly the refugees begin to think about returning home (Hammock and Charny 1996: 116).

According to Hammock and Charny, the relief agencies are perfectly content to see the replay of the morality story: 'they love it because they and their staff are invariably the heroes . . . Rarely is a critical glance cast in their direction. By definition, they are noble' (Hammock and Charny 1996: 116). But in their willingness to play along with the 'morality story' conventions, the relief agencies are complicit in the misrepresentation of the very crises that they seek to try to help resolve. Hammock and Charny contend that the standard script serves to misrepresent the complexity of humanitarian emergencies. Not least, the script makes what was avoidable and unnecessary seem completely natural and inevitable. The script transforms the social and historical into the natural in three ways. They all make it impossible to ask questions.

First, the morality play narrative makes it difficult, if not impossible, to analyse the root cause of the crisis. The disaster is presented first and the questions about why it happened are asked only later. The result is that, 'there is a strong tendency to view all emergencies as if they were the equivalent of natural disasters, beyond the control of people' (Hammock and Charny 1996: 117). According to Hammock and Charny, as soon as a disaster is presented in this way, as like a natural occurrence, the major problem becomes one of helping those who are suffering. The child is already starving to death, and so the main question becomes not 'how did this happen?' but 'how can we help the child?' In this way, the disaster is transformed into a logistical exercise in humanitarian relief. The news becomes the speed and efficiency of the relief effort. This further attenuates the naturalization of the disaster because it means that those who are suffering and miserable become identified as people to whom things happen (they are like natural objects), and all of the ability to act is identified with the Western relief agencies (who become the subjects who are resolving the problem that the victims cannot sort out for themselves). Hammock and Charny argue that: 'The definition of the problem merely as a logistical exercise puts the helper at the center of the process and treats the person to be helped as the dependent victim' (Hammock and Charny 1996: 117–18; this sentence is emphasized in the original). And so, once again, suffering becomes their fate and destiny. It becomes an inevitability if not, indeed, the nature of the Family of Man.

The second and third ways in which Hammock and Charny believe that the script naturalizes the suffering can be discussed more quickly, since they go beyond the specific concerns of this book and address wider issues about the politics of humanitarian aid. They also move beyond the description of what does happen and towards prescriptive statements about what Hammock and Charny believe ought to happen. Second, the script of the morality play never challenges the credibility of the relief agencies. The script casts 'a halo over every relief agency'. Yet 'the media must begin to ask hard questions about the actual credibility and capacity of agencies to respond to a particular crisis' (Hammock and Charny 1996: 118). Third, the script ought to try to denaturalize the power relationships which it otherwise all too readily takes for granted. In the standard script, Africans and Asians are people who are helpless without the relief efforts of the West. Hammock and Charny point out that the situation in the field is rarely so simple; local agencies are invariably in place, struggling to help long before the West is even aware that there is a potential problem. This leads Hammock and Charny to suggest that, 'the fundamental story of emergency response should always begin and end with the tremendous courage of suffering people to struggle against their situation and create a new life and new possibilities' (Hammock and Charny 1996: 119). However, the cynic might ask whether a convention which always concentrates on the 'tremendous courage of suffering people' is not itself a kind of morality play and therefore myth.

Why should the conventional story be changed? After all, even Hammock and Charny tacitly admit that the morality play narrative is effective insofar as it leads the audience to make financial donations to the relief agencies. For Hammock and Charny, however, the narrative should be changed because it promotes compassion fatigue: 'As disaster follows disaster, each following the same script, the public, whose support for the agencies is vital to their survival, loses its capacity to distinguish one disaster from another and one agency from another'. The victims become responsible for their suffering, nothing can be done to help, and the audience ceases to care (Hammock and Charny 1996: 116).

Like Barthes, what Hammock and Charny want is a refusal to accept that suffering and misery is ever inevitable, the way that things are, and natural. For different reasons, and within the context of very different analyses, they both want the world to be presented 'as it is' and without resort to comforting myths. But the rather more ambivalent position of John Taylor throws up the possibility that if we throw out the bath water of myth we might also be throwing out the baby of the possibility of compassion towards the suffering and miserable other. Taylor seems to realize (perhaps despite himself) that even though reports and representations are tied to conventions and do tend to naturalize that which is in fact social and historical, they are nevertheless capable of making the audience feel that the suffering other is making a moral demand. In other words, it can be suggested that it is precisely through naturalization (because of myth) and the 'human community' that it might imply, that the media are morally compelling.

The terrible irony is that the insistence on the historicity of the suffering and misery that is reported and represented leads to a collapse of moral universalism into a condition of incommensurability. Even though it might well be a 'myth' to uphold notions of moral universalism, with its associated referent of a universal human being and condition, the point nevertheless remains that these narratives make it possible for media audiences to feel compassion across and irrespective of constructions of race or ethnicity. To insist on the history of the suffering and misery (and to point out that some groups are always the sufferers while others are always simply the viewers), is to divide universal humanity and, therefore, to put humans into socially and culturally created categories. Those categories are rational and reasonable in their own terms, but it is impossible to find any neutral point of arbitration between them. Such a neutral point can be offered by the myth of a universal humanity, but that is exactly what is denied.

An emphasis upon the social and cultural history of the suffering and miserable was an important theme in some of the critiques which were developed of the Live Aid phenomenon in the mid-1980s. Live Aid initially emerged as a response to television news reports of the 1984 famine in Ethiopia. It took the form of charity fundraising records and concerts (featuring predominantly white pop and rock stars, for some of whom Live Aid was the launch pad for extraordinarily rewarding careers). To a considerable extent Live Aid was the precursor of many of the telethons which have become such a common feature of television programming in subsequent years. (For the background to Live Aid, see Harrison and Palmer 1986. For a quaintly *Marxisant* analysis of Live Aid, see Edgar 1985.)

In the wake of Live Aid, Anne Simpson (1985) wrote an article which developed a critique of some of the advertising strategies that were being used by Western charities such as Oxfam to try to get funds for famine relief. She started with a rejection of the view that famine is natural. Furthermore she argued that the claim that humanitarian aid is a solution to the problems of the Third World is fundamentally racist. Simpson insists on history. Arguments which deny history are predicated 'on a potent racist myth: that the crises of Third World countries are caused by lack of Western seeds, tractors or experts; and that their poverty is due to their own inadequacies'. This 'racist myth', according to Simpson, 'projects Third World people as helpless victims and Westerners as saviours, neatly ignores the fact that Western agents created the basis for underdevelopment in the first place . . . and that they continue to profit from that same underdevelopment'. The myth also denies that people in the Third World are capable of helping themselves, without Western intervention (Simpson 1985: 21). She argues that charity advertising is complicit in this myth and therefore in the identification of the Third World as a place of dependent victims. The advertisements and aid agency publicity mean that, 'Empire, debt, transnational corporations are written out of history' (Simpson 1985: 23). According to Simpson, this explains why images of children are so popular. The high profile that is given to pictures of children serves to confirm the helplessness and dependency of the Third World: 'the constant representation of Third World people through images of children means that, like the white missionaries before them, the donors can bask in the powerful position of adult in relation to child' (Simpson 1985: 22).

Of course, many of Simpson's analytical points are perfectly valid. She is absolutely right to emphasize the history of underdevelopment which makes the Third World so prone to consist of places of suffering and misery. Furthermore, it is legitimate to highlight the pain and exploitation which was perpetrated by those very Western nations which protest most loudly about moral universalism. But what positions of the kind which are exemplified by Anne Simpson's essay manage to achieve is little more than the introduction of a condition of incommensurability into the meanings and meaningfulness of reports and representations of suffering and misery. Simpson develops a coherent and sensible case from the initial historical premise that the problems of the Third World are largely due to deliberate underdevelopment promoted by the West. She develops her critique of advertising and aid publicity on the basis of that initial premise. This is clear when Simpson writes of the charitable representations that, 'These observers of misfortune have taken up the White Man's Burden and, in the manner of Victorian philanthropists, they have made charity a substitute for political change'. She goes on: 'In the blur of doing good and saving lives, the causes of poverty are ignored, and a fundamental solution postponed yet again'

(Simpson 1985: 25). Meanwhile, the charities and aid agencies whom she critiques develop a coherent and sensible case from the initial premise that the problems of the Third World have a significance from the point of view of commitments to moral universalism. The charities and aid agencies, in the first instance at least, rely on a myth of the universality of a human community rather than a history of oppression. They develop their fundraising strategies on the basis of that initial premise. And, as with all conditions of incommensurability, the problem is that it is impossible rationally to arbitrate between the 'historical' and the 'mythical' premises. In their own terms they are both rational and reasonable.

The 'CNN effect'

The 'morality play' conventions of the reporting and representation of suffering and misery (which are also revealed by Anne Simpson) might well be mythical, and it might be thought that it is beneficial to dismantle the idea of moral universalism in order to emphasize the differences which characterize humans. But, irrespective of these issues surrounding the conventions, what cannot be doubted is that they allow the audience to feel some kind of connection with the others on the page or screen. Those others might well be misrepresented, but still the audience is able to see that they are there and still the audience is able to recognize their suffering and misery as morally significant and compelling. This is because the conventions make the reports and representations predictable. The audience does not need to spend too much time gathering the details in order to know what is needed. It might even be said that the reports and representations, insofar as they exemplify conventions, establish what amounts to a moral shorthand about the world. They make it possible to recognize suffering *as* suffering. They stand for a kind of literacy and moral competence. (In this context it is worth recalling some of the points which were made by George Alagiah and mentioned in Chapters 1 and 2.)

However, the reports and representations tend not to inhere in time, but they are viewed and read one moment, and then they are gone. This is one of the issues that has to be addressed by any discussion of the moral compulsion of the media. The audience might feel that the picture of this or that dying man makes a demand, but the audience also knows that the photograph will have disappeared tomorrow and that the television report will be replaced by another in a minute or so. The demand that the man might make does not last very long. The feelings of shame and guilt, love and sorrow which are the basis of the lifting of the lid on the compassion of the audience dissipate almost as soon as they are stimulated. The point might not be that the compassion of the audience is fatigued, but rather that it is never really stimulated in the first place. This potential lack of stimulation is not due to the failings of photographers and reporters and neither is it due to the hard-heartedness of the audience. It might be woven into the nature of the media themselves. Morality play narratives and other conventions represent attempts to overcome this problem of the fleetingness of the coverage of suffering by reducing it to a generic shorthand. The problem is, however, that the conditions and the script of the shorthand might be changing.

This opens up the issue of the so-called 'CNN effect'. The concept of the 'CNN effect' is in fairly widespread usage. 'For many years commentators have drawn a connection between photographs of starving children on the evening news and a more aggressive U.S. policy to combat starvation, even to the point of military intervention – the CNN effect' (Natsios 1996: 152). Indeed: 'In its crudest form the CNN effect suggests that policy-makers only respond when there are scenes of mass starvation on the evening news. It also suggests that policy-makers obtain most of their information about ongoing disasters from media reports' (Natsios 1996: 150).

The phrase 'CNN effect' seeks to refer to the impact that 24 hour, rolling news services (such as the American Cable News Network) have upon news coverage. It implies that the increasing speed and immediacy of coverage has a direct impact upon the decisions of policy makers in the West. The nub of the debate about the CNN effect can be expressed in three propositions that are commonly made about it. First, it is often proposed that rolling news services make it possible for the news of the world to be broadcast extremely quickly; the news can be reported as it happens, without having to wait for the next scheduled bulletin. Consequently, the news can have a greater immediacy. Second, a considerable number of media professionals and commentators believe that rolling news services result in a certain shallowness of coverage since journalists have to spend most of their time before the cameras and can rarely, if ever, go into the field to find out the stories for themselves. Third, rolling news services tend to be broadcast via satellite technology. They are not nationally specific and can be watched anywhere in the world, possibly in 'real time'. It is supposed that, in this way, boundaries of time and place are transcended.

The impact of 24 hour rolling news was discussed by Jane Standley of BBC News at a conference on 'Dispatches from Disaster Zones', which was organized by the Reuters Foundation and held in London in 1998 (Standley 1998; all quotations from Standley are from this source. It should be noted that Standley herself did not use the phrase 'CNN effect'). Standley was in little doubt that, in the specific case of BBC coverage of the humanitarian crisis in Zaire which followed on from the genocide in Rwanda in the mid-1990s, rolling news had considerable benefits over scheduled reports. She used this experience as a base from which to look towards what rolling news might come to mean for broadcasters.

First, she argued that the proliferation of news programmes means that it is easier for a broadcaster to take on a 'big story', to discuss it from a variety of angles and to broaden the agenda of discussion. Second, Standley said that the demands of rolling news can lead to the establishment of news teams, 'so that everyone shares their information and knows what's going on, and we keep the viewer properly informed'. Third, and implicit to her argument, is the belief that the audience will increasingly turn to the Internet as a news source and, therefore, mainstream broadcasters will have to improve the quality of their news coverage in order to retain viewers. Standley is hinting that new technology will mean the improvement of news.

But Standley was also keenly aware of the problems which will emerge in the near future. She refused to get carried away by the potential of rolling news. First, rolling news means that coverage can be almost instantaneous and it can certainly be very thorough (after all, new news is always needed). According to Standley, this 'tyranny of real time' puts journalists at risk. She pointed out that every news report was 'watched and listened to in Zaire for example, or by the Rwandan government . . . you're still standing there, having just said your piece . . . and then the Zairean secret police used to come round and put you in gaol, and then expel you'. Standley went on: 'We are very, very exposed, we have our own lives and the lives of the people that we're trying to help to protect, but this is going to be more and more of an issue as these continuous news formats come on line'. This is because 'we're all going to be exposed to how we work being seen by the protagonists in a war, while we're standing literally right next to them'. If that comment highlights a direct physical threat to the journalist, Standley also mentioned the view that rolling news carries an intellectual risk in that the reporter will be under so much pressure to say something to the ever-present cameras that she or he will simply talk nonsense. (Standley attributes this position to the BBC reporter Fergal Keane, but it is also expressed very strongly by Martin Bell; see Bell 1996a.)

It has to be admitted that the idea of the 'CNN effect' does have an intuitive validity. Purely at a common-sense level, it seems obvious that if we in the West (and in particular if policy makers in the West) are able to watch a starving child die in real time then we are going to want to go to considerable lengths to try to alleviate the suffering. This situation is quite different from the one with more conventional news broadcasts and technologies, when it is possible to watch the pictures of the starving child with a fair degree of certainty that she or he is already dead and therefore beyond help and hope. But analysts who have tried to find evidence of the 'CNN effect' have cast doubt on whether or not it can be said to prevail.

One such analyst is Andrew Natsios. He has examined whether there is an identifiable 'CNN effect' behind American responses to humanitarian crises such as war in Somalia. At a first glance, the evidence is incontrovertible. It is historically obvious that American responses to suffering and misery in Africa or Asia have become more interventionist in the period since CNN came to be an influential force in international news reporting (that is to say, since the early 1990s). Is this merely coincidence? Natsios thinks that it probably is. He is certainly confident that the so-called 'CNN effect' is much more complex than the crude models might suggest. He reaches this conclusion on the basis of a study of the relationship between media coverage of humanitarian disasters (notably the war in Somalia in the mid-1990s) and US State Department policy decisions. The study leads Natsios to claim that, 'the CNN effect is of limited consequence, at times playing a supportive but not central role, and at others being a major factor in the decision-making process' (Natsios 1996: 152).

According to Natsios, whether the CNN effect has a supportive or major role is due to factors beyond its own control. This leads him to outline three propositions. First, Natsios says that American policy makers will respond positively and quickly to humanitarian disasters if the emergency threatens the geopolitical interests of the United States. In these circumstances: 'Electronic and print media attention will be tangential or irrelevant to the decision, whether or not the United States intervenes' (Natsios 1996: 153). Second, in areas of peripheral geopolitical interest to the United States, the initial response will be made by the US Agency for International Development if resources are available. 'Print and electronic media attention will be tangential or irrelevant in the initial response, but may influence sustained funding from Congress' (Natsios 1996: 157). Third, any American involvement in a crisis in an area that is entirely marginal to its interests will be opposed by officials if that intervention requires the use of military force, United Nations approval or diplomatic leverage on other countries. In these circumstances: 'The electronic media can play an important role in focusing public and policy-makers' attention to the crisis' (Natsios 1996: 159). The implication seems to be clear. There is no independent 'CNN effect' and, indeed, the media are influential in causing governments to intervene in disasters and crises only if that government thinks it is in its own or the national interest to so intervene. According to Natsios: 'The CNN factor may have consequences for fundraising for **NGOs** [non-governmental organizations] and for sustained congressional funding but is not essential

to early intervention except where troops for security are critically important' (Natsios 1996: 163).

But that is to assume that the introduction and establishment of rolling
news and global technologies serve to keep the audience better informed
about the problems of the world. The audience will feel that 'something
ought to be done' only if it is aware that there is a pressing problem in the
first place. And some commentators are sceptical about whether the audience is, in fact, better informed, simply because it has more and faster news
outlets at its disposal. For example, the American journalist Edward R.
Girardet has said that, 'I am not convinced that we are in any way better
informed today than we were during the 1960s or 1970s'. This is 'Despite
having far greater access to an overwhelming surfeit of information sources
than ever before' (Girardet 1996: 45). He says that even though there has
been a proliferation of news sources, 'Attention spans are shorter and one
can only absorb so much'. There is not enough time to take in all the news
that is available for us to see, hear and read. We rely on a small range of
trusted news sources such as a single newspaper and one or two television
channels. 'Even then, such diversity remains the domain of a tiny majority.
The majority of Americans, and increasingly, Europeans, turn to television
as their main, if not sole, source of news and current events' (Girardet 1996:
46). The problem is that television news is increasingly inward-looking,
decreasingly concerned with the world beyond the nation. According to
Girardet: 'Even though CNN . . . purports to be the world news channel, [it]
presents a far less cosmopolitan menu on its U.S. domestic network than the
one offered globally'. This is despite modest moves towards a broader based
coverage: 'Although CNN began broadcasting portions of its international
service to Americans at the beginning of 1995, the overall tone remains
highly parochial' (Girardet 1996: 47).

This problem of the limiting of horizons is not specific to CNN or American audiences, however. Similar charges can be laid against British media
institutions. For example, Jennie Stone (2000) has argued that British television has drastically reduced the amount of coverage it gives to the developing world. She says that the coverage has decreased both quantitatively (in
terms of the amount of air time) and qualitatively (the developing world has
become little more than the home of exotic species of animals). According to
Stone, the reasons for this decline include diminishing budgets for overseas
news; new technology which, while it allows for the quick and cheap trans-
mission of images, also leads to less in-depth analysis and commentary; and
increasing staff mobility due to changing relationships and structures in news
rooms (Stone 2000; this final point links the discussion back to the sociology
of the field of journalistic production which was discussed in Chapter 2).

Consequently, there is no necessary connection between the new techno-
logical means to broadcast the news of the world to the world and the moral
compulsion of broadcasts. The fact that suffering and misery in any part of
the world *can* be broadcast to a Western audience which might feel compassion towards the others does not mean that such reports and representations *are* broadcast. Furthermore, the time that is spent *watching* suffering
does not necessarily translate into time spent *with* suffering. It does not at
all follow that we *are* more knowledgeable about suffering and misery
simply because we *can* be more knowledgeable.

Conclusion

What should be clear from all of the above is that it is valid to suggest that
the media *can* lift the lid on the compassion of the audience. It can lift the
lid to the extent that reports and representations stimulate the moral feelings
of shame and guilt, love and sorrow. But there are a range of preconditions
for that stimulation to occur which are realized only contingently. There is
no *necessary* link between the report or the representation and the perceptions and feelings of the audience.

This chapter has sought to examine those preconditions as well as cast
some light on precisely why they are uncertain. It has been shown that positive photographs, preferably of smiling children, or logically compelling text
about the resolution of suffering and misery can be highly effective ways of
stimulating the feelings of shame and guilt, love and sorrow of the audience
(insofar as that stimulation can be measured through average financial
donations). Here, the precondition is the apprehension on the part of the
audience of an ability to have a positive impact upon the lives of others. But
this precondition is rendered contingent as soon as doubt is cast upon the
validity of the intimation of a universal human condition which links us all
together, irrespective of whether we are the potential donor or the potential
sufferer. Feelings of shame and guilt, love and sorrow, are predicated upon
apprehensions of a common humanity, yet those apprehensions can easily be
undermined through the revelation of the extent to which they are nothing
other than myths. With that revelation, the social and cultural – the *historical* – differences of human beings come to the fore. This carries the benefit of greater honesty but perhaps at the cost of denying any possibility of
action on the basis of a commitment to an ideal or assumption of moral universalism.

The chapter has also mentioned the ramifications of the development
of rolling news and real time broadcasting. It would seem that such

developments will have a considerably greater impact upon the field of journalistic production than it will upon the moral compulsion of the media from the point of view of the audience. Girardet makes the important point that it does not follow that more information means being better informed and the study by Natsios shows that there is a fundamental paradox about any 'CNN effect' (even in those relatively few situations in which such an effect can be identified as a significant variable factor).

Indeed the conclusions of Natsios seem to imply the opening up of a gulf between the feelings of the audience in the face of reports and representations of suffering and misery and the likely responses of governments. An awareness of this gulf is implicit to Natsios's appreciation of the possibility that the 'CNN effect' can have an impact upon fundraising from the public but that it is only coincidentally influential upon the actions of policy makers. This throws up the problem of the moral action of the audience. The audience might well feel that certain reports and representations are enormously morally compelling. But there is little it can do to help alleviate the suffering and misery. The audience is not in the field hospitals and neither does it have the logistical capacity to deliver food or other aid to those in need. And policy makers will press the button for those kinds of responses to be put in hand only if, according to Natsios, they identify such a response as being in the national interest. Where there is no geopolitical interest in an area, then the suffering and misery that is experienced there is likely to be the cause of little or no relief effort, irrespective of the feelings of the audience. The audience will be able to engage in moral action only if it works outside and around the spheres controlled by the established policy makers.

And that is to point towards the concerns of the next chapter.

Further reading

Barthes, R. (1972) *Mythologies*. (Trans. A. Lavers.) London: Jonathan Cape.

Dyck, E.J. and Coldevin, G. (1992) Using positive vs negative photographs for third-world fund raising, *Journalism Quarterly*, 68(3): 572–9.

Rotberg, R.I. and Weiss, T.G. (eds) *From Massacres to Genocide: The Media, Public Policy, and Humanitarian Crises*. Washington, DC: Brookings Institution and Cambridge, MA: World Peace Foundation.

Simpson, A. (1985) Charity begins at home, *Ten: 8*, 19: 21–6.

Taylor, J. (1998) *Body Horror: Photojournalism, Catastrophe and War*. Manchester: Manchester University Press.

TELETHONS, INVESTMENT AND GIFTS

Introduction

One of the major problems for the audience is that, as soon as it feels moved into action by the reports and representations of the suffering and misery of others, it has to hand over control of the levers of response. If the lid on my compassion has been lifted by shame and guilt, love or sorrow, the difficulty I face is that actually there is nothing I can do to help. I might feel strongly that 'something has got to be done', but I cannot do it and the most I can achieve is to make a donation to one of the relief agencies or charities that *are* able to do something. The problem is that however moved I might be, I do not have the logistical support or the technical competence (even less the physical proximity and the time out from the worries of my own life), that would enable me actually to save any lives at all. The best I can do is find a proxy who will act on my behalf. Then again, insofar as relief agencies and charities are themselves involved in a struggle for the finite financial resources which the audience might be encouraged to supply, I will not have to look too hard to find a proxy. They will, instead, come looking for me. And because I know the names of these organizations and have seen and read about their previous work, I will be more or less happy to give them the resources to act on my behalf.

When the proxy is an arm of the state, the resolution of the problem of the inability of the audience actually to 'do something' for itself might not be so straightforward. As Natsios's (1996) investigation of the 'CNN effect' demonstrates, states intervene in humanitarian crises only when they perceive that specific geopolitical interests are at risk. In these terms, the feelings of the audience tend to be of a largely secondary importance. The state will support them (and, for that matter, encourage them) only to the extent that the compassion can be used to legitimize or bolster an intervention which would have probably been carried out in any case. An example of such a happy coincidence of geopolitical interest with the compassion of the audience is almost certainly provided by the NATO decision to bomb Serbian troops in 1999, in the name of helping Kosovar refugees and discourage the 'ethnic cleansing' which the Serbs were carrying out.

But the other side of this equation is, of course, that circumstances can arise in which the compassion of the audience has been stimulated by reports and representations of suffering and misery and yet the state (as the proxy actor *par excellence*) has no intention whatever of intervention. This situation is almost certainly illustrated by the gap which frequently emerges in the wake of coverage of a terrible occurrence like the genocide in Rwanda in the mid-1990s. The genocide was widely broadcast and reported, and it is not unreasonable to suggest that the professionals of the field of journalistic practice were actually very competent in communicating the enormity and horror of what was happening (contrary, perhaps, to di Giovanni's account of compassion fatigue). However, in terms of the responses of the Western states at least, there was negligible intervention because few geopolitical interests were being challenged. Similarly, at a first glance the bombing of Chechens in 1999 by the Russian army raised the same ethical issues as the Serbian bombing of Kosovars a few months earlier and yet, as was widely reported at the time, there was no hint of state intervention precisely because no geopolitical interests were being threatened.

When there is this kind of gap between the moral sensibilities which are stimulated by the media and the likelihood of proxy action by the state, actors tend evidently to develop their own forms of mobilization. They begin to operate around and irrespective of the state in order to try to ensure that some relief work is carried out. A number of analysts have placed a great deal of emphasis on this operation around and independently of the state. They have identified it as something approaching the birth of a new politics. In this vein, Michael Ignatieff has written that since 1945, a combination of 'affluence and idealism' has led in the West to 'the emergence of a host of nongovernmental private charities and pressure groups . . . that use television as a central part of the campaigns to mobilize conscience and money on behalf of endangered humans and their habitats around the world' (it is worth noting how that sentence unintentionally makes humans sound like tigers or pandas. This is a resonance that commentators like Anne Simpson or Jennie Stone would undoubtedly stress, albeit for different reasons). The bodies about which Ignatieff talks include Oxfam, Amnesty International,

Save the Children and Christian Aid. According to Ignatieff, these voluntary bodies represent the emergence of 'a politics that takes the world rather than the nation as its political space and that takes the human species itself rather than specific citizenship, racial, religious, or ethnic groups as its object'. He says that this is, 'a "species politics" . . . It is a politics that has tried to construct a world public opinion to keep watch over the rights of those who lack the means to protect themselves'. The instrument of this 'new kind of politics' is television (Ignatieff 1998: 21).

Meanwhile, Martin Shaw has sought to assess the validity of the thesis that the media representation of distant violence has led to the audience feeling a certain responsibility towards the suffering other in such a way that it might be possible to talk about a new terrain of civil society (Shaw 1996). To this extent he might almost be interpreted as offering a case study in the validity of Ignatieff's more essayistic and speculative contentions. When Shaw addresses the issue of representation, he uses the word 'representation' in a specific way, and in a way which is quite different from how it has been used in this book. For our purposes, 'representation' has meant a likeness or an image. This is a fairly simple definition which brushes aside important epistemological and ontological questions, but it is perfectly sufficient for our purposes. When Martin Shaw talks about 'representation' he means advocacy and political influence. It is in these terms that he links the representation of distant violence to civil society, since 'Civil society is held to comprise the institutions which have the specific role of *representing* groups within society, in broad cultural, political and ideological senses, both in the context of society itself and in relation to the state' (Shaw 1996: 13).

This definition of representation means that when Shaw wants to understand how distant suffering is represented, he has to try to find organizations and voluntary bodies which carry out a measure of advocacy on behalf of the miserable. For Shaw, the interesting possibility is that, given that the media operate on an increasingly global terrain, it is logically permissible to wonder if organizations and voluntary associations are similarly able to develop across national boundaries. It is undoubtedly with these kinds of possibilities in mind that, in his discussion of civil society, Shaw talks about, 'its world-wide expansion, the decline of some traditional national forms and the rise of global (or globalist) social movements, NGOs and media' (Shaw 1996: 15).

These possibilities were assessed by Shaw through empirical studies of English media audience responses to coverage of the Gulf War of 1991 and the subsequent humanitarian crisis in Kurdistan, and the war in the Balkans in the early to mid-1990s. He actually found little evidence of a global civil society: 'apart from media and humanitarian agencies, there was little evidence of effective responses to the Kurdish crisis. There is little to suggest anything different in any other crisis' (Shaw 1996: 175). For Shaw, the nub of the matter was that if there are traces of a global civil society then the English media audience he studied should have been participating in certain political relationships which would have been representing (advocating) the case of the suffering and miserable. Yet he found that the English audience would tend to express concern for the victims of distant violence only if that suffering possessed some national angle. For example, the English audience worried about the Gulf War in 1991 because British troops were present, but it remained relatively unconcerned about the crisis in Kurdistan or the later suffering in the Balkans because there was no British involvement. Consequently, despite what the media might imply, there was little or no evidence of a movement of the horizons and associations of civil society beyond the terrain of the nation state.

Shaw looked for the signs of a global civil society and failed to find them. In these terms, his conclusion is extremely unsurprising. Shaw seems to take the absence which is implied by his empirical study to be a sufficient justification for the claim that there is *no* advocacy for the suffering apart from that representation which is carried out by the usual groups and institutions (the media and humanitarian agencies). He concludes that a global civil society remains to be established. His book ends with a call for such a civil society across and beyond national boundaries: 'It is necessary to transform institutions in national civil societies with globalist thinking, to awaken and strengthen feelings and concepts of global responsibility' (Shaw 1996: 182. It is worth noting that Shaw's reference to 'awakening' and 'strengthening' notions of global responsibility presupposes that the audience is *already* possessed of a certain moral universalism).

From motivation to investment

Both Ignatieff and Shaw identify the action which is carried out by the audience with a participation in politics. Ignatieff uses a fairly loose definition of politics which is expanded to include everything that the audience does, ranging from fundraising for charitable causes to protesting against state policies. Meanwhile, Shaw has a somewhat narrower, and on the face of it more clear, definition of political action. He links it with the participation of the audience in the voluntary associations of civil society. But neither of these identifications really comes to grips with the problem of explaining in detail exactly why it is that the members of the audience feel that such political action is necessary and appropriate. That is, they both tend to underemphasize the question of *motivation*. Of course, neither Ignatieff nor Shaw ignore this matter entirely. For Ignatieff, the audience is motivated by the history of compassion and, in particular, by its moral universalism. Meanwhile, Shaw argues that the audience is motivated by a fairly complex sense of responsibility which establishes the need to represent the suffering and misery of others (Shaw 1996). Yet if it is agreed in the light of Gilligan's work that compassion is not some single and unitary emotional response to suffering, and if it is also agreed that any sense of responsibility might be inflected by the differences of the moral voices of justice and care, then the conclusion has to be that Ignatieff and Shaw tend to oversimplify.

Moreover, a conceptual or analytical focus on the *politics* of moral compulsion leads to a tendency to ignore the distinct possibility that the forms and genre of media reports and representations are themselves likely to have an impact upon how the audience might respond to any given disaster or crisis. Once again, however, it would be wrong and unfair to say that analysts like Ignatieff or Shaw ignore this issue entirely. Certainly, Ignatieff has paid it some attention, although it has to be said that his reflections are not terribly able to deal with the complexity and differences of audience apprehensions of moral compulsion and of the morally compelling.

The great strength of Ignatieff's approach is that it refuses to see the media and its audience in isolation. Moreover, and by implication rather than by express statement, he also makes it possible to analyse media reports and representations in terms of how and to what extent they manage to communicate the concept of moral universalism. Consequently, Ignatieff offers something by way of a healthy alternative to those approaches that focus their analytic horizons *exclusively* on the form and representations of the media. But there is also a weakness at the heart of his thesis. The problem is that Ignatieff's assumptions tend to be overly rationalistic. Running through Ignatieff's essay seems to be an assumption that the audience will feel moved by certain pictures and stories because they are the subjects of the long history of European moral universalism. However, Ignatieff goes on, the audience will not be so moved as and when the media do not allow them to spend time with the suffering of others (this is a problem which is lent some weight by the claims of Girardet which were discussed in Chapter 4). As such, Ignatieff leans towards the conclusion that the most morally compelling reports and representations will be those over which the audience can linger and spend time with that suffering other. This leads him to call speculatively for the scrapping of the genre of television news and, instead, its replacement with documentaries: 'If the nightly news were replaced by magazine programs and documentary features, the institutional preconditions for a journalism that respects itself and the terrible events it covers would begin to exist'. This is because 'The best documentaries sometimes achieve the prerequisite of moral vision itself; they force the spectator to see . . . and to encounter alien worlds in all their mystery and complexity'. He says that, 'There is almost never an occasion when the time formats of news bulletins allow even the best journalist to do the same' (Ignatieff 1998: 32. Here then, think of the case of George Alagiah's reports from the Sudan, mentioned in Chapter 1).

What is wrong with that conclusion, and the reason why it is overly rationalistic, is that it is predicated upon the assumption of an unproblematic connection between the media and the audience. Ignatieff takes it for granted that if television (the focus of his concern) begins to broadcast programmes that can express a moral vision, then the viewers of those programmes will be reminded all the more of the extent to which they are the subjects of the history of moral universalism. And so, Ignatieff assumes, those viewers will then begin to conduct themselves according to the dictates of that moral command. They will refuse to accept the excuses of nation states that nothing could be done about this famine or that war, and they will begin to make more sizeable donations to the relevant charities. He assumes a direct relationship between the cause and the effect. Unfortunately, social relationships, and most certainly moral conscience and action in the context of the recognition of the suffering of others, does not seem to obey the dictates of rational and direct relationships. This is precisely the point that Chapters 3 and 4 of this book were seeking to establish.

Ignatieff tends to assume what might be called a 'direct flow' model of the connection between television and its audience. Within his assumed model, television and its audience are connected by the flow of information from the former to the latter and by the action that the latter engages in because of the former. In other words, Ignatieff empties the space between television and its audience of any influence and effect. That assumption of an empty space, filled only by the flows that enter into it from either end, is unable to capture the social and cultural dimension of the relationship between television and its audience. Ignatieff's television audience might well be constituted by and as the subjects of a history of moral universalism, but he does not take his treatment of the social and cultural situation beyond that claim. Perhaps it is this *under*socialized account that explains why Ignatieff argues that the moral significance of television can be radically transformed by the relatively simple expedient of the broadcasting of different genre of programmes.

The question that needs to be asked, and the question which neither Ignatieff nor Shaw are well placed to answer (since they both concentrate on a politics which is conceptualized as nothing more than the effect of a cause initiated by the media), is that the audience does not respond equally and identically to all reports and representations of suffering and misery. There is a difference. But what *makes* the difference? Part of the answer to that question (a part which has not been addressed so far in this book), involves the ability of the report or representation to compel an *investment* on the part of the audience.

Investment and leisure

The concept of investment has been taken from a study by Martin Barker and Kate Brooks of 'fandom' in relationship to cinema films (Barker and Brooks 1998). In particular, Barker and Brooks studied how a group of fans of the *Judge Dredd* comics approached the film of the same name which was released in 1995. Obviously, we are not about to take a massive diversion into a full and detailed discussion of Barker and Brooks' research findings (and, in any case, were that diversion to be carried out, it would be significantly less engaging and absorbing than Barker and Brooks' own discussion). Their study is interesting for our purposes of trying to understand why it is that the audience engages in action consequent upon some reports and representations of suffering and not others, because it tries to confront a parallel problem of explaining the different engagements of *Judge Dredd* fans with the film. Barker and Brooks tried to explain why some fans paid attention to all stages of the film-making process and got involved in detailed discussions about movie production and the star system, while others went to see the film in a far more apathetic state, for 'something to do'. They offer the concept of investment in order to try to understand these kinds of differences of attitude, commitment and engagement.

According to Barker and Brooks, the movie fans 'are choosing the extent to which they will participate in forms and fields of their culture. We've chosen to name this dimension of caring and committing oneself to a particular orientation, the process of investment' (Barker and Brooks 1998: 225). They make the point that these choices are themselves the outcome of social and historical processes. It should be becoming clear already that this concept of investment is helpful for our purposes. What we have got to try to explain is the extent of the participation of the audience in the suffering and the misery of others. We have got to explain how and why the members of the audience make the choices that they make. So far, in Chapters 3 and 4, we have seen that the choices that are made by the members of the audience might well feel to them to be natural and beyond debate (because compassion is so centrally tied in with the other directed personality type which is presently the social and cultural dominant), but that, actually, these attitudes towards suffering and misery are the outcome of a history of moral sensibility. That history can be understood as a social and cultural process in which social actors have been 'trained how to respond, and to participate. They have to learn the "rules" (of efficacy, of success, of aesthetics). They have to learn to participate "properly", that is, with a proper orientation of both mind and body' (Barker and Brooks 1998: 226).

Moreover, as Chapter 3 sought to stress, it is legitimate to make the theoretically informed speculation that dimensions and meanings of 'caring and commitment' (to use Barker and Brooks' phrase) are likely to vary according to whether they are structured around and in terms of the moral voice of justice or care. Barker and Brooks state that, 'This concept of "investment" . . . is intended to summarize all the ways in which audiences demonstrate strength and depth of involvement to a social ideal of cinema' (Barker and Brooks 1998: 225). If the word 'cinema' is replaced with 'media', and if the phrase is read only in the context of the specific problem of moral compulsion and significance, then the concept of investment continues to hold good and to have considerable analytical purchase. What it opens up is an investigation of the relationship between the media and the audience which does not collapse into some presumed 'direct flow' model of cause and effect or which assumes that either pole (media or audience) can be discussed in isolation from the other. The concept requires us to begin to ask questions about how an ideal of what the media ought to do (ideals which are represented and justified by the field of journalistic practice which was explored in Chapter 2) interrelates with the 'strength and depth of involvement' of the audience.

Now, Barker and Brooks found that those members of the audience who upheld a strong ideal were also likely to demonstrate a fairly determined and focused kind of investment, whereas those who had a less strong ideal were more likely to adopt a mixture of orientations. In substantive terms, this means that those fans who had a strong ideal of what a *Judge Dredd* movie should be like were very prone to invest heavily in the film. They would make sure that they knew all about its production, they would hold conversations about it and would vividly remember the film. By contrast, those fans who had a less strong ideal were also less strong investors. In the extreme case of low ideal and low investment, Barker and Brooks found people who 'do not care, they do not invest, they do not remember' (Barker and Brooks 1998: 225). Barker and Brooks pull together the meanings and resonance of 'investment' when they write that the concept, 'references the differences that are made according to how much people care about their participation or involvement'. They continue to say that, 'high investment . . . [is] associated with greater and more detailed preparation for the activity, with a more concentrated but selective manner of attending and participating, and with a greater capacity for disappointment'. Meanwhile, 'Low investment . . . is associated with less focused and less retentive ways of participating. And people who are low investors seem to have very much less to say about their involvement' (Barker and Brooks 1998: 229).

By extension, it can be proposed (with, as ever, due caution), that those members of the audience who uphold an ideal of objectivity for the media will tend to be high investors in those reports and representations which are possessed of the legitimacy of objectivity and impartiality. They will be able to talk about the report or representation and, it can be speculated, they are likely to approach it as something that, actually or potentially, might be apprehended as morally compelling. Meanwhile, those members of the audience who uphold an ideal of sensationalism and human interest will tend to be relatively low investors in reports and representations which rely on their objectivity and, it can be speculated, they are likely to be prone to become easily bored and unmoved. This is one theme that might be able to lend some greater sociological plausibility to the compassion fatigue hypothesis. By this analysis, compassion fatigue could be interpreted sociologically as a reflection of low investment. In the case of the high investors, it is likely that an orientation of action will be taken toward reports and representations of distant suffering and misery, while in the case of the low investors it is likely that an orientation of curiosity or boredom will be more evident. The high investors will run between the poles of enthusiasm and disappointment, the low investors will stand in the middle, not moved too much either way. And all of this raises questions: 'How important is it to them [i.e. the audience], and why? What do they hope to achieve through their participation (and that notion of "hope" reintroduces our idea of ideals)? In what kinds of organization (informal, formal; narrow, wide) do they embody the manner of their participation?' (Barker and Brooks 1998: 229). These are the kinds of questions that we also need to ask (see note 1).

These questions also highlight the key problem that media professionals have to be able to resolve insofar as their production can be fractured between the competing and irreconcilable aims of objectivity and the sensationalist demands of market. The productions have to be able to uphold the ideal of the high investors in the audience whilst also appealing to the ideal of the low investors. More substantively, media productions have to be able to facilitate action and participation on the part of those who look for seriousness and entertainment alike. This explains why Ignatieff's conclusion about a new moral seriousness emerging from the simple expedient of changing genre of reporting is inadequate and why Shaw looks in the wrong place when he tries to find the emergence of a globalist civil society. They both ignore the sociology of investment. And that sociology can go a considerable way towards explaining why and how it has been that moral compulsion so often gets translated into the leisure pleasure of the audience.

The translation of morality into a leisure time pursuit warrants some consideration before the discussion can proceed. This translation is one of the keys to understanding the moral action of the audience, and yet it is totally missed by the likes of Ignatieff and Shaw. There are two reasons why they miss this peculiar and yet defining feature of how the audience 'does something'. First, Ignatieff concentrates on the amount of money that is raised by charitable appeals. For example, when he talks about the action that ensued from the news reports of the famine in Ethiopia in the mid-1980s and which were the stimulus for the Live Aid movement, Ignatieff seems to feel that it is appropriate to establish the importance of the television broadcasts of the famine with the comment that, 'In Britain alone, more than sixty million pounds was donated to famine relief agencies' (Ignatieff 1998: 10). In this way, no attention whatever is paid to the action by and through which that sum was raised. This is a consequence of his implicit 'direct flow' model. Second, Shaw concentrates on the voluntary associations of civil society and thus reduces moral action to political representation. To put it simply, Shaw seems to take it for granted that serious issues are met with serious responses. But that assumption makes it impossible to glimpse the specificity of the action that the audience performs. If it is all reduced to the emergence of a politics of a globalist civil society, then it is all flattened and any chance of analytic precision is ruled out.

Of course, there is an obvious explanation why moral action is a leisure pursuit. It could be argued that this translation has occurred for the simple and straightforward reason that it is only in their leisure time that social actors become aware of suffering and misery through the media and, moreover, that it is only in their leisure time that they have the opportunity to 'do something'. But there might be much more to be said than that. Chris Rojek opens up an interesting line of thought when he comments that, 'modern life creates constant anxieties about the nature of our real feelings' (Rojek 1993: 212). It is not unreasonable to suggest that Rojek's point can be illustrated by the condition of moral incommensurability which has been identified as a crucial component of the situation of the audience (and the reasons why the audience *as* audience can act morally but not ethically). Certainly social actors have real feelings when they are confronted by reports and representations of the suffering of others, but because of incommensurability, it is difficult to know what those real feelings are or how they might be spoken about. As the work of Gilligan can be taken as implying, it is quite likely that whatever discussion there is will be carried out in terms of different moral voices, thus creating even more anxiety and confusion. Rojek goes on to claim that: 'The person today who constantly worries about who he or she is, or how he or she should act to do good in the world is seen as being too serious. Intensity betokens introspection and this can be unattractive to others' (Rojek 1993: 212). The point which can be added to this observation is that, if it is accepted that contemporary character is largely other directed (this was, to recall, one of the arguments that was made in Chapter 3), then the 'person today' will be desperate to try to look attractive, not unattractive to others.

If the two themes which are opened up by Rojek are pulled together, it becomes possible to reach an answer as to why it is that moral action has been translated into a leisure time activity (and, by extension, it is also possible to appreciate why a globalist civil society is very unlikely to emerge; unlikely, that is, assuming that the theoretical speculations of this book are taken to be valid). First, social actors (the members of the audience) do experience 'real feelings' (or, at least, their feelings are experientially real) insofar as they are the subjects of a history of moral universalism and, moreover, to the extent that they have necessarily experienced the dramas of attachment and separation which are typical of childhood. These feelings lead to an orientation towards the suffering and misery of distant others, although the precise nature of that orientation is variable. Second, incommensurability means that those 'real feelings' cannot be assumed to be universally shared. As soon as they are expressed they might well lead to conflict rather than agreement. They might result in the exclusion of the individual from social relationships. An anecdotal illustration of this possibility is provided by the doubts which tend to be expressed about people who 'wear their heart on their sleeve' or the condemnation of 'do-gooders'. But, given that the individual social actor is also an other directed character type, exclusion is a threat which must be avoided at all costs. This is because exclusion from social relationships is tantamount to an assault on self-identity.

Consequently, 'real feelings' will tend to be expressed in an unserious manner insofar as seriousness implies introspection, and introspection is possibly unattractive to others. And the *more* 'real' the feelings are experientially, the *more* they will tend to be expressed in an unserious manner. Hence, it can be speculated, the translation of the serious business of morality into leisure time entertainment. Hence, also, the validity of our extension and application of the concept of investment. Perhaps there is not too great a distance between moral action and leisure entertainment at all, and that the contemporary connection of the two should not cause any great surprise.

Telethons

One of the strengths of the concept of investment, and therefore of the refusal to assume some 'direct flow' model of cause and effect between the report and representation and the audience, is that it can begin to make some sense of one of the other most significant peculiarities of the moral action of the audience. The action is not just a leisure pursuit. It is a *particular kind* of a leisure pursuit.

Nearly all of the existing debate about suffering and misery and the audience gives primacy to the genre of news. Ignatieff and Shaw provide excellent examples of this tendency. They talk about news reports only on television or in the press. They tend to ignore any and all other kinds of coverage. Furthermore, the entire debate about compassion fatigue stresses only the exhaustion of the moral sensibility of the war reporter and photographer or the weariness of the audience in the face of the relentless stream of the news of suffering and misery. But it is noticeable that, even if news can be identified as the initial spur for the moral action of the audience, as soon as that action emerges there is a more or less rapid shift of the significance of the suffering and the misery of others into the forms and genre of light entertainment. Analysts like Ignatieff and Shaw imply a very realistic state of affairs, in which the audience responds to serious news in a serious and sober way. The point is, however, that seriousness and sobriety emerge only some times and, quite probably, with decreasing frequency.

Instead of the hard political work of the forging of some globalist civil society (assuming, that is, that the concept of civil society is held to be useful; perhaps Shaw presumes something which needs to be justified: see Tester 1992), the moral action of the audience tends to be associated rather more with the pleasures and fun of the telethon. It can be speculated that this is because, unlike the kind of politics in which Ignatieff and Shaw place all their hopes and conceptual awareness, the telethon is remarkably able to secure, maintain and regenerate, the investment of the audience, irrespective of whether the members of that audience are high or low investors.

One of the few academic discussions of the telethon is provided in a very useful article by Eoin Devereux (1996). The article is at once an introduction to the genre of the telethon and a study of how the *People in Need* telethon in the Irish Republic represents poverty. Devereux amplifies and contextualizes his study of the telethon in his book *Devils and Angels* (Devereux 1998. His book contains the article to which I have referred as its Chapter 4; my pagination of citations from Devereux refer to the article, not the book). Devereux makes it possible to become aware of, first, exactly what it is that might be labelled as a telethon and, second, the history of the genre.

So, how can a telethon be identified? The very word 'telethon' can be unpacked to provide some initial clues. The first part, 'tele', makes it plain that telethons are not generic to the media as such but are, instead, the peculiar property of television (with radio and, increasingly, the Internet, operating as little more than supporting players to the central player of television). The second part, 'thon' comes from the word 'marathon' and indicates that the broadcast is not a passing affair but, instead, lasts a long time and requires commitment and dedication. Consequently, a telethon is a lengthy television broadcast. In terms of content, the telethon asks the audience to support a specific charitable cause or to address a particular range of suffering and deprivation by pledging donations by telephone or participation in specially organized events. In these terms, it can be seen that telethons require at least two kinds of *investment* on the part of the audience; time and money.

But, more substantially, Devereux offers a number of points by way of distinguishing the telethon from other kinds of television broadcasts. According to Devereux, telethons typically mark the 'entry of television into a fund-raising role'; override and suspend normal programming; are extremely lengthy; involve the participation of celebrities; rely upon the corporate sector to donate goods and services; have a considerable amount of audience participation; offer 'the opportunity (theoretically at any rate) to gain greater insight . . . through the use of filmed segments and interviews'; stress the ability of charity and charitable donations to resolve the relevant problem; place 'great emphasis on the (heroic and sometimes unusual) activities of individuals, groups and communities who have raised money for "good causes"' (Devereux 1996: 48). As well as Devereux's case of RTE's *People in Need*, the BBC's *Children in Need* appeal is, therefore, a prime example of a telethon, as is the biannual *Comic Relief* effort.

Although telethons are now widespread phenomena, they are an American invention. Devereux notes that the Jerry Lewis Telethon in the United States has long been a feature of American television. It introduced the world to this particular type of programme. Broadcast annually every Labor Day (Devereux 1996: 48–9), the telethon raises funds for the Muscular Dystrophy Association. It was first broadcast in 1966 by one station in New York but, despite that originality and limited reach, still managed to raise more than $1 million for the charity. It was the first telethon to 'go global' when in 1998 it was broadcast via the Internet. The show lasts for about 22 hours and secures a huge audience. The telethon website quotes audience figures of 25.5 million households in the United States with an estimated 64.1 million adult viewers. (All of this information is from the MDA Telethon web pages at http: //www.mdausa.org/telethon).

As Devereux (1996) notes, the first telethon in Britain was produced by London Weekend Television in 1981, but the genre had to wait until Live Aid in 1985 before it really took off: 'Seen worldwide by millions of viewers, this spectacular televised rock concert raised millions of pounds for the starving and destitute of the developing world'. Devereux suggests that Live Aid communicated three dominant messages. First, it suggested that the starving in Africa have been let down by existing structures. Second, that charity represents a solution (although not, perhaps, a sufficient solution) to the problems of the Third World. Third, that the media 'whether it be through the record/music business or through television, radio and newspapers [have] a role to play in attempting to alleviate poverty and inequality through fund-raising' (Devereux 1996: 49). Valid as these observations are, they nevertheless miss out on what was, perhaps, the dominant message of Live Aid: remedying the problems of the world (that is to say, moral action oriented towards the suffering and misery of distant others), need not be dull and boring. It can be fun and exciting. Live Aid turned morality into a leisure time entertainment, a transformation that has been pushed ahead, in Britain at least, by both *Comic Relief* and *Children in Need*.

For his own part, Devereux speculates that the telethon is a successful genre because, unlike news or documentary reports and representations, it involves the cleansing of suffering: 'in telethon television, the images we see of poverty and need are sanitized and relatively invisible in the wider context of a programme which emphasizes entertainment and fund-raising'. Devereux wonders whether 'the telethon is often more about the audience themselves as opposed to the objects of their charity' (Devereux 1996: 64–5). Such a suggestion, which is based on a careful study, resonates with Bauman's claim, which was mentioned in Chapter 1 of this book, that the strangers in the telecity are present only in an aestheticized form and thereby denied of any aspect of an ability morally to compel. As we shall see later, there is another basis upon which it might be possible to agree with Devereux's suggestion that the telethon is more about the audience than the sufferers. Meanwhile, through the concept of investment, it is possible to add further dimensions to the attempt to understand the popularity and undoubted success of telethons.

Telethons are able to appeal to high and low investors alike. For the former they provide insight through the film clips which are shown through the course of the evening. To this extent, telethons can be approached as primarily serious forms of broadcasting which have the wrapping of entertainment only in order to ensure that the campaigning and fundraising does not come across to the other directed characters as being *too* serious. In this way, the high investors are able to intimate that they feel deeply and engage passionately with a cause while also demonstrating their ability to 'have a good time'. Meanwhile for the latter group, for the low investors, the meanings of the telethon are likely to be reversed. They are likely to be attracted to the entertainment content of the broadcast and to pay the clips about the relevant charity relatively less attention. Yet in this way, the telethon producers are able to gain an audience even among those individuals who would not otherwise participate in or donate to charity appeals and, in so doing, there is a maximization of the pool of potential donors. Unlike many other genre of broadcasting, therefore, telethons are able to gain an audience among those who would be likely to watch in any case as well as among those who would be extremely unlikely to watch more conventional forms of charitable appeal.

Spurs to investment

Within the telethon format itself, it is possible to identify three spurs to investment.

First, the telethon indicates that, however great the suffering and misery, 'something can be done', even by those individual social actors who in all other respects rely on the proxy actors of the state or the humanitarian aid and relief agencies. Devereux makes a helpful insight in this respect. Although his paper focuses on an Irish telethon which seeks to raise money for the relief of poverty in the Irish Republic (and, therefore, even though his empirical focus is not precisely on distant suffering and misery), he nevertheless shows that the short films within the telethon are of enormous significance. These short films seem to play a dual role. They do not just offer an insight into the problem at hand. They also indicate that 'people like us' can make a positive contribution even if, as in Devereux's study we know no poor people ourselves, or even if we have no personal contacts with famine victims. Devereux points out that in the Irish telethon, these short films lasted a grand total of only 11 minutes and 4 seconds and, although some of the films were repeated, he reaches the conclusion that, 'it is clear that the programme's primary function was to focus on the activities of the helpers of the "deserving" and not on the "deserving" themselves' (Devereux 1996: 61). In the films, 'a great deal of time was given over to those who are working either on a professional or voluntary basis for the poor or needy'. Just as importantly the films represented the helpers (who Devereux calls the 'agents of the poor') and the poor themselves in quite contrasting ways. The helpers were given an identity, the poor were denied one: 'Those who are the agents of the poor are shot speaking to camera, while the poor themselves are shot in silhouette' (Devereux 1996: 61).

The conclusion that it is possible to pull out of Devereux's interesting observation is that, through this emphasis on the helpers at the expense of those who receive the help, there is the attribution of a certain activity to the audience. They are shown that people just like them are able to make a difference in the world, and that distances can be overcome through purely personal effort. The moral world thus is reduced to a sphere which the individual can influence (and, in so doing, political, social or cultural causes of poverty or other kinds of suffering and misery are pushed far into the background). In this way, the guilt which is associated with the moral voice of justice is assuaged through the intimation that part-time (and therefore not necessarily overly intrusive on the self) attachments can create a fairer world (and perhaps this is why the films focus on the 'deserving' as opposed to the 'undeserving'). Meanwhile, the sorrow which is associated with the moral voice of care can be turned into a happiness and joy of attachment.

From all of this it is possible to propose that telethons are able to secure investment through their ability to make the world of suffering and misery make some kind of coherent and ready sense. The poor and destitute cease to be a troubling challenge and, instead, they become silent victims who are always with us. In other words, they are made to make sense through strategies of naturalization (and so the discussion of myth in Chapter 4 becomes relevant). Once again, Devereux makes the point well. He says that the telethon 'offers the powerful a role to play as benign figures who help those who are relatively powerless. This serves to ensure that the status of those who help out are reaffirmed and not questioned in any way' (Devereux 1996: 65). The logical corollary of this point is that if the lot of the suffering and miserable is therefore put beyond question, the actions of the audience are made into the main cause of anything happening in relation to those who are the recipients of the charity. Certainly, then, suffering and misery may well be natural and inevitable, but it is only natural and inevitable for those who are represented and reported. Those who watch are, on the contrary, implicitly identified as agents (and so the film segments in telethons might be read as scenes in the wider morality play of humanitarian relief). In this way, investment can be secured once again. The high investors will be given the sense that they can make a difference and the low investors will be given, at the very least, a sense of relative well-being and prosperity.

But to return to the three spurs to investment within the telethon format. Second, it is worth considering the role of the celebrities in the telethons. What exactly do they do? Of course, there is the obvious answer that the celebrities front telethons for the simple reason that they are recognizable and experienced presenters. In this way, low investors will be attracted either because they like the celebrity or because there is some kind of a guarantee of an entertaining show. High investors, meanwhile, will probably identify the presence of the celebrity as a vindication of their own feelings and sensibilities. The celebrity will be a representation of the possibility that experientially deep feeling does not necessarily imply introspection and the kind of inwardness which other directed characters seek to avoid in others. This implication will be all the greater if the celebrity comes from the world of comedy or music. Then it will be possible to believe that experientially deep feeling goes hand in hand with an ability to please, and to be pleasing to, others. The celebrities are figures who appeal to the concern of the other directed character with authenticity and the social validation of deep feelings. In a different yet comparable context, the sociologist Robert K. Merton once commented on Kate Smith, one of the most successful celebrities in the American War Bond campaign of the Second World War: 'For many, she has become the symbol of a moral leader who "demonstrates" by her own behavior that there need be no discrepancy between appearance and reality in the sphere of human relationships' (Merton 1949: 145). This is exactly the kind of demonstration that the other directed character – beset with deep feelings which can be expressed only at the risk of social disapprobation – craves to see in others.

Third, telethons secure investment because they connect the other directed character with a community of seemingly similar individuals. In this way, telethons imply an overcoming of the status of television viewing as an activity which tends to take place in the domestic sphere, and in the family unit. Telethons connect the particular domestic sphere to a much broader set of relationships. For example, one of the typical features of a telethon broadcast is the time it devotes to events from one's local region. The national broadcast is frequently suspended so that television viewers can get details of what is happening in their neighbourhood. On the one hand, this serves to imply that the whole nation is united and has pulled together. Differences of region, economy or accent are subordinated to the inclusiveness of a national community which is able evidently to be compassionate when given the opportunity (but, of course, this intimation of the national community is largely mythical in the Barthesian sense of the word 'mythical'). On the other hand, the local items serve to bring the enormity of the telethon down to a personal scale. Given the frequency and geographical distribution of the local items, it is not unreasonable to imagine that one will see a friend (or the friend of a friend) on the screen, participating in some event or other. Consequently, the spectacle of the telethon is lent a personal validity and dimension. The national telethon ceases to be enormous, the nation itself becomes something to which the individual social actor can, and wishes to, connect and with which she or he is able to engage. Therefore, a lack of willingness to participate might be read as an indication of an individual who is too introspective to be prepared to 'help others', and too unable to 'have a good time'.

For all of these reasons, the telethon can be interpreted as the definitive genre for the translation of the moral sensibilities of the audience into action. The telethon is uniquely placed to be able to secure the attention of high and low investors alike. This is because the genre is at once focused enough and yet flexible enough to be able to accommodate different interpretations and degrees of attention. In these terms, it would be perfectly wrong to contend that those who watch the telethon only to laugh along with the celebrities are carrying out some kind of 'resistance' in relation to the form. They are not. They are, much more simply, just low investors in the ideal of moral compelling television. Similarly, it is quite wrong to reach the conclusion that those who avidly watch the film segments and then phone in with a cash card donation are the dupes of the voluntarization of welfare provision or of the privatization of overseas aid. Rather, it is more constructive (and, for that matter, much less arrogant) to identify them as the high investors in the ideals of compelling objectivity in relation to the suffering and misery of distant others. These are individual social actors who take extremely seriously the ideal of solidarity which follows from any conception of moral universalism.

However, the further significant point which needs to be made about the genre of the telethon is that it is able to secure the attention of high and low investors alike on a *recurrent* basis. Certainly, telethons are not monthly phenomena, but they are frequently annual (or at the least frequent, they are biannual), and still they are able to secure an audience and participants. This is a state of affairs that the compassion fatigue thesis would find it difficult to understand and explain. After all, if the thesis is right, then it would be expected that the audience would become decreasingly large and decreasingly likely to make donations as telethon follows on from telethon. Yet this is precisely not what seems to happen. Telethons are able to secure investment over and over again. The question is: how?

As ever, the question has an obvious and a slightly less obvious answer. The obvious answer would say that telethons secure recurrent investment on the part of the audience for the simple reason that telethons generate only a finite sum of money and that the money, by its very nature, will shortly be consumed. By this answer then, telethons have to happen annually or biannually because the money runs out, and the audience invests according to the same calendar on the basis of the presentation of new film clips of suffering and misery or new entertainment items. The conclusion which is reached if this line of thought is followed through is that telethons start with a clean slate. But that answer is not tenable because part of the appeal of a given telethon is precisely the fact that this broadcast stands in a line with the one last year and from the year before that. It would seem to be the case that telethons 'deliver the goods' in no small part because individual social actors in the audience are able to know in advance what is required of them and, moreover, the uses to which the donations will be put.

The telethon actively plays on this continuity and to some extent actually needs it for the format to flourish over time. One of the main components of any telethon broadcast is the recurrent announcement of the running total of donations that have been received. Whenever the amount is announced, the audience is invariably reminded by the celebrities of the sum which was raised last time around. That enforced recollection is unlikely to be interpreted by the other directed social actors in the audience as a simple statement of facts. It is much more likely to be interpreted as a goad since they will not want to seem to others and themselves to be less caring and compassionate than the audience of last year or two years ago.

So, contrary to everything that the compassion fatigue thesis might lead us to expect, it seems to be appropriate to suggest that the telethons are able to secure recurrent investment *precisely because of their predictability*. This predictability has a number of dimensions. First, and as we have already seen, the predictability is in part due to the fact that the audience already knows what is going to be demanded prior to the demand of the telethon actually being made. Second, it can be suggested that the telethon is predictable because it manages to reduce suffering and misery to 'bite size' segments in which the victim is distanced from the audience by the emphasis upon the helper. Third, telethons are predictable in the sense of the calendar. They are a central and constitutive part of what might be called a 'national calendar' of moral concern (compare Rojek 1993: 42). This 'national calendar' means that the audience knows that it will have certain demands made of it every March (for example) or, to put the same argument much more cynically, it means that the audience always and already knows that it need show explicit concern for suffering and misery only for a couple of days every year.

In all of these ways, telethons are a significantly more important form of broadcasting than news, at least in terms of their ability to cause moral action on the part of the audience. Of course, news can be morally compelling and significant. This ability was seen very clearly in March 2000 during the coverage of the floods in Mozambique (which, it ought to be noted, fitted exactly into the script of the 'morality play' that was discussed

in Chapter 4). News broadcasts devoted great time to reports and representations of people forced to live for up to nine days in tree-tops, and after
a week of such coverage, appeals were broadcast, fronted by celebrities,
asking for donations to be made to the relevant humanitarian relief charities. But the overt compassion which was stimulated towards the people of
Mozambique did not last long (exactly as Arendt's discussion of compassion
would lead one to expect). The overt care was fleeting. It was not recurrent
beyond a couple of days. Why?

Undoubtedly, the compassion quickly dissipated for all of the reasons that
the compassion fatigue thesis would stress. The news quickly became
boring, the problem started to get sorted out, different events were pressed
upon the audience and so forth. But it is much more fruitful to analyse the
dissipation in terms of the problem of the securing of recurrent investment.
News broadcasts, left to themselves, are unable to secure recurrent investment. It can be suggested that this is because they too *quickly* have an impact
upon high investors (who are likely to make their donation within minutes
or hours of being asked, and who then have little or nothing left to do) and
too *weakly* have an impact upon low investors (who might never watch
them in any case). Telethons avoid falling into these two traps since they are
so very predictable.

The gift of money

Yet there is another important aspect of the moral action of the audience
which warrants more than a cursory analytic glance. The discussion of
telethons has frequently referred to the fact that through the genre, the audience is enjoined to make money donations. As we have just seen, it is always
the case that the appeals which are based on news reports and representations also boil down to the same request – send money. The audience is
never asked to give up its jobs in order to go to the disaster zones and very
rarely is it asked to start writing letters to put pressure on the government.
The audience is never enjoined to create some 'globalist civil society'. Instead
it is appealed to as a collection of individuals, each of whom can act independently in such a way that deep feelings need not be revealed to others
who might laugh but who, in fact, almost certainly share the same sensations. The audience is always asked simply to make a donation, either by
credit card or by visiting a bank or post office.

Obviously, that kind of appeal reflects the realities of humanitarian relief
work. It also reflects the fact that the media audience acts in the disaster
zones only through a proxy. To this extent, money is all that the audience

can give. Moreover, it is perhaps best that this is all the audience give since, not to put too fine a point on the matter, were members of the audience parachuted into the flood or war zones it is improbable that many of them could be of any terribly great help. Some things are best left to the professionals. However, if we think about the donations less as a simple act and more as a kind of social relationship, then the significance of the requests for money and the subsequent donations becomes a lot more interesting. In particular, if the donations are considered in terms of a social relationship, then it becomes possible to analyse them as a *gift*.

The sociological importance of the gift was stressed long ago by the French anthropologist Marcel Mauss. He understood gift relationships to be absolutely foundational to social solidarity. According to Mauss, it is possible to identify three aspects of gift relationships: 'the obligation to give, the obligation to receive and reciprocate' (Mauss 1990: 39). Mauss explains that the obligation to give is derived from a social necessity to demonstrate good fortune. This obligation is a constraint upon the individual and to deny it is to put oneself outside of social relationships (Mauss 1990: 40). Second, the obligation to accept the gift is due to the fact that to refuse to accept it is to exclude oneself from the social: 'To act in this way is to show that one is afraid of having to reciprocate, to fear being "flattened" . . . until one has reciprocated . . . It is to "lose the weight" attached to one's name. It is either to admit oneself beaten in advance or, on the contrary, in certain cases, to proclaim oneself the victor and invincible' (Mauss 1990: 41). These two dimensions of the gift relationship come together when Mauss writes that, 'to refrain from giving, just as to refrain from accepting, is to lose rank – as is refraining from reciprocating' (Mauss 1990: 41). Third then, Mauss talks about the obligation to reciprocate. To fail to give something back to the donor of the gift (or, as Mauss makes plain, to refuse to destroy something of at least equal value to the gift) is, once again, to challenge the ties that constitute the basis of social solidarity: 'The obligation to reciprocate worthily is imperative. One loses face for ever if one does not reciprocate' (Mauss 1990: 42).

Mauss derived his account of the gift relationship and its centrality to social solidarity from an anthropological study of other societies. But he was in no doubt that the form of this relationship can also be seen in contemporary, Western, social relationships. He was quite clear that, 'A considerable part of our morality and our lives themselves are still permeated with this same atmosphere of the gift, where obligation and liberty intermingle'. When he wanted to illustrate this claim, Mauss started to talk about charity and he pointed out that charity is a gift which is given without the overt intimation of an obligation to reciprocate. In this way, charity makes the recipient of the gift socially lower than the donor. Mauss says: 'The unreciprocated gift still makes the person who has accepted it inferior, particularly when it has been accepted with no thought of returning it'. Indeed, 'Charity is still wounding for him who has accepted it'. According to Mauss, however, it is possible to identify in contemporary charity an attempt to overcome this intimation of the greater prestige of the donor in relation to the recipient (Mauss 1990: 65). Yet is this the case in the specific instance of telethons or, more broadly, in the case of audience donations in order to relieve distant suffering and misery?

In order to answer that question, it is first of all necessary to confirm that Mauss's dissection of the gift relationship can be applied to the moral action of the audience. That confirmation can be secured if the relationship between the audience and the suffering and miserable other is dismantled along the lines of Mauss's three dimensions of the gift relationship. First, it is necessary to identify the basis of the obligation that the donors feel towards the recipients. This is derived from the history of moral universalism and, perhaps much more importantly, from the moral voices of justice and care. The voice of justice will lead to feelings of guilt that it is unfair for 'us to have so much while they have so little'. Meanwhile, the voice of care will lead to feelings of sorrow that 'everything they have has gone'.

Second, it is necessary to identify the obligation to accept the gift. Of course, part of the obligation is derived from sheer material want but there are at least two other aspects of the obligation. First, the suffering and miserable are not able to refuse the gift since it is, in the case of sacks of grain or rice, simply dumped in front of them from helicopters bearing film crews who fly away immediately after the drop has been made. Second, and relating back to the critiques of the representation of want in charity appeals (see the discussion in Chapter 4), the suffering are identified by the donors as in no position to refuse the gift because they are taken to be unable to look after themselves (and, thereby, any such refusal is interpreted by the donors as a mark of insolence, bad faith or a lack of obligation in the future). Third, it is worth thinking about exactly what it is that the recipients give back to the donors. What are the relationships of reciprocity?

As ever, let us begin with the obvious answer. The gift relationship expresses the reciprocity of social solidarity. The donor makes a gift to the recipient and the recipient gives something back to the donor. As such, the purpose of the gift is a demonstration and a practice of social solidarity. It is impossible to resist making a link from Mauss to Ignatieff since Ignatieff is talking about nothing other than the nature of the solidarity between the audience and the suffering others who are reported and represented by the media. In these terms, money is a gift that is able to overcome the great gap that separates the imaginative and moral closeness that is implied by narratives of universalism, from the geographical and substantive distance that is implied by presence on a newspaper page or a television screen alone. To this extent, it could be suggested that money is a gift that leads to the repayment of the donors with a re-establishment of the solidarity of a community of humanity even though that solidarity is fractured by distances and even though doubt has been called upon any narrative of universality by the critique of myth. In these terms, the gift is humanity itself. That is what the suffering others repay to the donors in this thoroughly mediated gift relationship.

However, a much more cynical explanation of what the suffering others give back to the donors is offered by Jean Baudrillard. His explanation also emphasizes the problem of the social and cultural particularity of the narrative of moral universalism upon which Ignatieff places so much of his hope. Whereas Ignatieff stresses how the narrative has led to the universalization of solidarity and, specifically, to the contention that humans are morally compelling precisely because they are human and thereby considered with compassion, Baudrillard rather more tends to point to the contemporary continuations of other narrative traditions, such as imperialism. Baudrillard gestures towards the claim that what the suffering of the others repay to the donors is a sense of the latter's moral superiority. In Baudrillard's terms therefore, telethons and charity are not simply about compassion and the solidarity born of universalism. They are more probably about condescension on the part of the audience. This is especially likely to be the case when the suffering others are inhabitants of the southern hemisphere.

Baudrillard makes these claims in the course of his book *The Illusion of the End* (Baudrillard 1994). He says that the South produces the raw materials that the North consumes, and that the most recent of these raw materials is catastrophe. What this means for Baudrillard, talking to his audience in the North, is that, 'We are the consumers of the ever delightful spectacle of poverty and catastrophe, and of the moving spectacle of our own efforts to alleviate it' (Baudrillard 1994: 67). Indeed, Baudrillard goes on to argue that, 'Our whole culture lives off this catastrophic cannibalism, relayed in cynical mode by the news media, and carried forward in moral mode by our humanitarian aid' (Baudrillard 1994: 68). In these terms, the reports and representations of the suffering of others can be treated as the replacements for the physical raw materials that the southern hemisphere used to provide but that the North has either exhausted or replaced. Now the South produces the raw materials of the good conscience of the audience, 'like coffee or other commodities' (Baudrillard 1994: 68). Or, as Baudrillard himself puts it: 'material exploitation is only there to extract that spiritual raw material that is the misery of peoples, which serves as psychological nourishment for the rich countries and media nourishment for our daily lives' (Baudrillard 1994: 67). The logical conclusion of Baudrillard's claims is therefore that what the recipients give back to the donors is their silence and their ability to be spoken for without having to be listened to, in exactly the way that Simpson's demythologizing critique of charity advertising would suggest.

Baudrillard's comments can lead the discussion back to Devereux's analysis of telethons. Baudrillard and Devereux rather tend to complement each other in that they both put question marks against precisely why it is that gift relationships are entered into by the audience. They question the meaning of solidarity and thereby the whole basis of the moral tie between the audience and the others. As Devereux points out, the telethon or charity appeal implies that this relationship is neither necessary nor compulsory since it 'reemphasizes the ideology of voluntarism which views the responsibility of solving problems such as poverty and need as being within the bailiwick of individuals, organizations or communities' (Devereux 1996: 66). This voluntarism about making a donation represents a clear break between the contemporary gift that is mediated through reporting and representation and the classic gift as it was uncovered by Mauss. For Mauss, the gift only *appears* to be voluntary; despite this appearance, the gift is in fact deeply tied in with a system of duties and reciprocity (Mauss 1990: 1). That is part of the reason why the gift relationship connects with the question of social solidarity. Yet Devereux points out that the gifts of money that are given by television viewers are not at all necessary. To that extent it becomes possible to suggest that the contemporary gifts cannot be connected with an *obligation* of solidarity. It becomes possible to suggest that instead they point towards an *option* and a *preference* for solidarity with the relatively distant suffering and miserable others.

The usefulness of Devereux's study is that it thereby makes it possible to connect the otherwise questionable speculations of Baudrillard – and for that matter Bauman – to an empirical case. Through Devereux it is possible to suggest that Bauman is right when he says that morality is aestheticized via television (Bauman 1993), and this leads to the conclusion that the financial donations will increase in direct proportion to the cleansing that aestheticization involves. The implication seems to be that the more the suffering of others is simply decorative, the more it will be likely to be the cause of a donation of money. The high investors will be struggling all the more frantically to try to find some depth behind the suffering while the low investors will simply be more and more entertained. It is also possible to suggest that Baudrillard is right when he implies a reworking of Mauss's gift relationship to ask what it is that the suffering strangers give back to the audience. Devereux rather points to the conclusion that Baudrillard is right when he speculated that what they give back is a sense of power, well-being and, essentially, an ability to look down upon others even though mythical narratives like imperialism or moral universalism itself have been cast into fundamental doubt and even though it is difficult to be completely sure about what compassion means.

Conclusion

We end up with the question which was the originating point for this book. What is the moral significance and compulsion of the media? One way in which that question can be answered is if attention is paid to Georg Simmel's essay which deals with the meanings of the metaphors of the bridge and the door (in Simmel 1997). Are the media like a bridge, or are they like a door? Although Simmel deploys his metaphors in terms of a treatment of the connections between the human and the natural worlds, what he says can be applied more or less directly to the question of the connections between the audience and suffering others, mediated through press and broadcasting.

Simmel begins his essay with the statement that, 'The image of external things possesses for us the ambiguous dimension that in external nature everything can be considered to be connected, but also as separated' (Simmel 1997: 170). The audience is connected to the suffering other on account of the history of moral universalism validated by feelings of compassion, but they are nevertheless separated by cultural, spatial and temporal distances as well as ontological divides. Yet Simmel goes on to contend that even when a separation is highlighted, that itself implies a connection of some sort: 'By choosing two items . . . in order to designate them as "separate", we have already related them to one another in our consciousness, we have emphasized these two together against whatever lies between them' (Simmel 1997: 171). In this way, this book has related to each other the separate groups of the audience and the suffering and miserable others on the page or the screen. More specifically, as soon as a question is raised about the moral compulsion of the media for the relationship between the audience and the suffering and miserable, those two separate categories are being connected because they are being focused upon, and the distances between them are being approached and considered in terms of whatever might connect them. For Simmel, that relationship can be understood through the metaphor of either a bridge or a door.

Simmel says that a bridge connects that which is separate: 'the bridge symbolizes the extension of our volitional sphere over space. Only for us are the banks of a river not just apart but "separated"; if we did not first connect them in our practical thoughts . . . then the concept of separation would have no meaning'. He goes on to say that where separation is identified, 'the spirit now prevails, reconciling and uniting' (Simmel 1997: 171). A bridge provides for movement from one shore to the other, and thus it connects that which is separate. It does not require too much stretching to apply this metaphor to the case of the media. It can be suggested that the media can be interpreted by means of the metaphor of the bridge insofar as they do indeed connect that which is separate. They create a kind of unity of humanity and, in so doing, they can be taken to provide a representational legitimacy to any conception of moral solidarity such as universalism. They also constitute a medium for compassion. The media as a bridge give an object, and therefore a moral integrity, to conceptions of moral universalism that, perhaps, serves to temper the implicit imperialism of any claims to speak for and on behalf of the unity of human being and which might also serve to mollify the bad faith that is revealed by Baudrillard and suggested by Devereux. Moreover, the metaphor of a bridge also emphasizes the movement from the one shore to the other. By extension therefore, it would allow for a focus on the *relationships* between the audience and suffering and miserable others rather than on the one at the expense of the other.

However, if the media are interpreted more through the metaphor of a door, then the situation becomes rather different. Whereas bridges connect, doors separate. As Simmel puts it, 'Thus the door becomes the image of the boundary point at which human beings actually stand or can stand' (Simmel 1997: 172). Now, Simmel points out that the door implies the 'possibility of a permanent interchange' between that which is inside and that which is outside, but the interchange will have different meanings depending on the direction from which one approaches it. The meaning of a door is different whether one is entering the space or exiting. If this metaphor is applied to the case of the media, a very complex picture of moral compulsion begins to emerge. On the one hand, the media can be interpreted as a door through which the audience enters into a much broader space of moral responsibilities and solidarity. This is the 'window on the world' understanding of the media. However, and on the other hand, if the media are interpreted as a door onto a world from which the audience is absent or has been offered the opportunity to exit (through morality play narratives and the like), then the media can be interpreted as a literal and metaphorical 'screen' between the individual social actor (and more broadly the audience) and all that is outside. In this case, the relationship between the audience and the suffering and miserable others is likely to be interpreted in terms of boundaries and limits; I am in here, they are out there. This is the situation that seems to be implicit to Bauman's image of the telecity and it explains why, in his account, the strangers on the screen have to engage in a struggle to get through to the audience. Moreover, this metaphor can also be applied to an attempt to answer the question 'why is money the gift?' In these terms, money becomes an agency of moral action precisely because it can go through the door without requiring any movement on the part of the donor. Money enables the screen to remain intact.

Yet if that last speculation is correct, perhaps the meanings of the gift of money fall into two categories. The first category of the gift will be a version of the classic Maussian type. The donors give money and are repaid with the promise of the moral solidarity of all human beings, despite social, historical and cultural factors. This might be called the mythical promise. But the second category is considerably less straightforward. If it is accepted that the media are like a door that keeps the donor and the recipient, the audience and the suffering and the miserable, quite apart from one another and consigned to separate bounded spheres, then perhaps the money is a free gift that is intended to discharge responsibilities without, however, creating a connection of any sort at all. By this account, what seems to be a recognition of a demand for solidarity based on the universalism of compassion is actually an avoidance of it. Mary Douglas has explained that, 'What is wrong with the so-called free gift is the donor's intention to be exempt from return gifts coming from the recipient . . . A gift that does nothing to enhance solidarity is a contradiction' (Douglas 1992: 155). Yet it by no means follows that gifts are *not* given in *exactly* the hope that they will do nothing to enhance solidarity.

Note

1 It is important to clarify a methodological point about the relationship between high and low investment on the one hand and the moral voices of justice and care on the other. *We can assume absolutely no direct mapping or identity of the one with the other.* Individual social actors whose compassion is shaped through justice can be either high or low investors in the media as a channel of moral communication, as can those individual social actors whose compassion is shaped through care concerns. It is necessary to recognize this principle since it reinforces the point that it is theoretically and methodologically unsatisfactory to assume that the media will be apprehended as morally compelling by all individual social actors in the same way. What this book has been trying to show is that monolithic theorizing is unsustainable and simplistic methodology is untenable.

Any empirical research which seeks to develop the kinds of themes which are raised in this book ought to have as one of its concerns an exploration of the precise relationship between the different moral voices and different levels of investment. That research should also seek to discover whether any correlations map onto social and cultural categories such as gender, age or class. Purely at a theoretical level, it is reasonable to expect that such research will, as Gilligan indicates, identify gender foci to the moral voices. It would also be important to address the correlation – or the lack of correlation – of a voice to a level of investment or, for that matter, of a given level of investment to categories such as gender, age, class and so forth.

Further reading

Barker, M. and Brooks, K. (1998) On looking into Bourdieu's black box, in R. Dickinson, R. Harindranath and O. Linne (eds) *Approaches to Audiences: A Reader*. London: Arnold.

Devereux, E. (1996) Good causes, God's poor and telethon television, *Media, Culture and Society*, 18: 47–68.

Devereux, E. (1998) *Devils and Angels: Television, Ideology and the Coverage of Poverty*. Luton: University of Luton Press.

Ignatieff, M. (1998) *The Warrior's Honor: Ethnic War and the Modern Conscience*. London: Chatto and Windus.

Mauss, M. (1990) *The Gift: Forms and Functions of Exchange in Archaic Societies*. (Trans. W.D. Halls.) London: Routledge.

Shaw, M. (1996) *Civil Society and Media in Global Crises: Representing Distant Violence*. London: Pinter.

CONCLUSION

The point was made at the outset that this is a book to be used rather than the statement of a position. It is more by way of an invitation to a dialogue than a coherent and unitary thesis which demands to be defended. That, at least, is the objective according to which the book has been written. And, given that objective, it would be inappropriate and misplaced for the discussion to end with a conclusion that ties up any threads of the argument that have been left dangling in the air (in any case, some of that pulling together was carried out in Chapter 5). All I want to do in this Conclusion is to recollect the most obvious features of where we have been on this journey and indicate some places that might be explored in the future.

In terms of where we have been, I hope it has been clear that the book has been written in the space between the broad parameters that were outlined in Chapter 1. In that chapter we saw that according to Alain Finkielkraut and Zygmunt Bauman at least, media reports and representations are, for a variety of reasons, unable to move the social actors who together constitute the audience. Finkielkraut and Bauman paint a picture of a world in which we all read the newspapers and watch the television and, for the most part, get quite extraordinarily bored. And let us be honest, it does all get a little bit boring doesn't it? In this book I have referred to horrors which have happened around the time of its being written, but I am perfectly confident that in the time between me writing this and you reading it, a whole catalogue of new suffering and misery has been compiled. But, as this book has sought to demonstrate, while the claims of Finkielkraut and Bauman might have enormous moral integrity and a high measure of polemical impact, there is good reason to suggest that they rather tend to overstate the matter. The social actors who read and watch the news do not always get bored, they (we) are not always left apathetic. We might be bored and apathetic a lot of the time but, sometimes, something happens which stirs us out of stupor and inspires us to take part in events like telethons. Sometimes some things make a difference. This book has sought to try to explain how the difference might or might not be made.

Yet we set another parameter in Chapter 1. We saw that journalists like Martin Bell, George Alagiah and Ed Vulliamy are utterly convinced that their work possesses a profound moral dimension and that it is incumbent upon themselves to tell their readers and viewers that dreadful suffering and misery are being experienced in the world. A central plank of their professional virtue is provided by their commitment to the belief that they have an incontrovertible and unqualified moral obligation to tell the audience what is happening to other people. And the journalists also believe that, insofar as they have been successful, the members of the audience should be outraged by what they have come to know, and begin to exert pressure so that something is done to alleviate the problem. In this way, the journalists assume a fairly straightforward model of the relationship between the media and the members of the audience, in which the members of the audience simply respond to the news that is put before them. But, as Alagiah and Vulliamy in particular were aware, the members of the audience do not always respond in the way that was intended. Sometimes the audience does nothing, sometimes it does quite a lot. And it would seem that it is impossible to predict audience action in advance. As such, some journalists blame themselves for failures to act and turn towards the explanations which seem to be offered by the compassion fatigue thesis. However, as this book has sought to show, the complexities of compassion mean that there is no reason for the journalists to blame themselves since the audience is an utterly independent constituency and the social actors who constitute it are beset with the kinds of moral dilemmas and difficulties which are thrown up by the condition of incommensurability. Or, put another way, perhaps there is no such thing as compassion fatigue because it is actually very difficult to say for sure what compassion means.

This book has involved a journey in terms of those parameters, a journey in which it is now possible to see that the parameters might well posses a lot of common-sense validity but, perhaps, they are best approached as polar opposites which are equally to be avoided. The complex relationships between compassion, morality and the media are much more played out in the muddy and murky middle.

So, if that is where the journey has taken us, where might it be useful and interesting to go in the future? Merely to ask that question is to assume that these kinds of issues will continue to be relevant and, unfortunately, there is no reason whatsoever to imagine that they will cease to be germane. Wars and violence, famines and floods, suffering and misery will continue to happen, and will continue to destroy lives and ambitions, until the end of all things. Consequently, it is worth pointing to a few areas in which it might be worth thinking about future research and analysis. Obviously, other areas will be added to this list as you work with this book for yourself.

First, it will be pertinent to examine the relationships of the field of journalistic production through the study of the culture, politics and economics of institutions of cultural production. If Bourdieu is right then it is likely that in the future, the authority of objective reporting will be eroded to such an extent that it is ultimately replaced with sensationalism and a focus on the human interest angle. That speculation itself logically leads to the expectation that reports and representations of suffering and misery will be either increasingly fleeting (they will not be dwelt upon over time because they will lose their sensationalist impact) or they will not be covered in the first place (because the audience might get bored, switch off and thus deprive the media source of its access to markets). What then happens to the virtues of journalistic practice?

Second, it will be useful to think about the impact that the media have on moral ties and feelings. Is it possible to continue to think about morality in ways bequeathed to us by philosophers and social thinkers who were scarcely if at all aware of television? Do the radically unique circumstances of the present require us to develop radically new and original ways of thinking about morality? Or does the present call upon us to recommit ourselves to the time-honoured codes and emotions of morality *precisely because* they are incompatible with what press and broadcasting imply? This is a historical-philosophical area of inquiry.

Third, text-focused analysis could usefully develop methods and procedures by and through which it might be possible to examine the relationships between different moral voices and degrees of investment. It would also be pertinent to seek to enquire whether there is a form of report or representation that is 'morally privileged' and more likely than other reports or representations to be taken by the audience to be morally compelling, or whether it is always and inevitably the case that reports and representations will be apprehended differently by the different moral voices of care and justice. Text-focused analysis might also pay attention to 'morality play' conventions in the reporting and representation of humanitarian disasters and seek to inquire whether they are a useful shorthand for mobilizing a quick response or whether, instead, they merely serve to naturalize the suffering of others.

Fourth, and finally, there is a pressing need for sustained academic attention to be paid to the form and implications of telethons. Telethons might well seem to be immensely trivial features of the world and, it must be said, watching them is not a terribly pleasant or edifying experience. And yet they are increasingly the means by which the social actors of the audience engage in action in order to try to 'do something' about the suffering and the misery of others. There is presently a hole in our knowledge about why actors participate in telethons. With the concept of investment, this book has sought to gesture towards one means for the study and analysis of the subjective meaningfulness of telethons. Within this sociological line of inquiry, it would also be valuable to consider the extent to which the telethon represents a continuation – or perhaps even a modification or a revocation – of the anthropological form of the gift.

These four areas of possible inquiry are, to say the least, huge. But if analysis is going to come anywhere close to responding to the demands which are made by suffering and misery, they point to a few of the issues to which we must dedicate ourselves.

GLOSSARY

Action: action can be of two kinds, social or non-social. Non-social action is entirely self-focused, and concerned only with inanimate objects. Action can imply the treatment of others as like inanimate objects insofar as there is a destruction or ignoring of their dignity independent of the actor. Social action, by contrast, involves an orientation on the part of the actor towards others as subjects possessed of their own, independent, dignity. Social action means taking others into account, regardless of whether those others are recognizable and known individuals or, in principle, simply indeterminate others who are identified as being compellingly significant by the actor. To the extent that the concept of the audience implies *social action*, and to the extent that social action means *taking others into account*, it can be concluded that the audience is a *moral constituency*.

Audience: the methodological ideal type which is constituted by and of those who read newspapers which have some commonality of content, and those who listen to or watch the same radio or television broadcasts. The newspaper readers and the broadcast listeners and viewers are not mutually exclusive groups.

Bystander's journalism: a phrase coined by Martin Bell to refer to that journalism which concerns itself dispassionately with the 'facts' and which involves no communication of personal feelings or emotions on the part of the journalist. It is journalism which is practised consciously in a tradition of objectivity and accuracy. Bell is critical of what he calls 'bystander's journalism' and contrasts it with the *journalism of attachment*.

Compassion:

> In languages that derive from Latin, 'compassion' means: we cannot look on coolly as others suffer; or, we sympathize with those who suffer . . . In languages that form the word 'compassion' not from the root 'suffering'

but from the root 'feeling', the word is used in approximately the same way but . . . with another light . . . a broader meaning: to have compassion (co-feeling) means not only to live with the other's misfortune but also to feel with him any emotion.

(Kundera 1984: 20)

In Gilligan's account of different moral voices, the voice of justice expresses the compassion of sympathy and the voice of care expresses the compassion of co-feeling.

Compassion fatigue: 'the feeling that world events are so distressing and thanks to the media we are so heavily exposed to them that as earthquake follows earthquake, and famine succeeds famine, each will blend into the other and the battered viewer will lose his or her ability to extend compassion to the myriad victims' (Green 1991: 56). However, the application of the phrase 'compassion fatigue' is not unique to audiences. It has also been applied to the dulling of the emotional sensitivities of journalists.

Compulsion: one dictionary definition of 'compulsion' refers to 'an irresistible, repeated, irrational impulse to perform some act, often against one's will'. This definition offers one way in which it is possible to understand how it is that media reports and representations of the suffering of distant others are identified by the audience as being compelling (that is, as being the basis of an impulse to act. That action is moral insofar as it implies *social* action). Compulsion is not the simple and direct consequence of any given, or any genre of, report or representation. Compulsion is the result of an interplay between the place of the report of representation in the field of journalistic practice; the extent to which it resonates with the history of moral universalism; the different meanings of compassion; and the strategies and determinations of the expression and securing of the investment of the audience.

Ethical: the standards of the right or good, or of how we ought to behave and act. Compassion is the basis of the dominant ethic (and most certainly of the dominant ethic in terms of the relationship between the audience and suffering others) in contemporary social and cultural relationships.

Incommensurability: 'What obtains when two or more groups assign different meanings to words, thereby . . . causing their sentences to be about different worlds and opening an abyss between their respective conceptual schemes' (Stout 1988: 295). In conditions of incommensurability, there is a plurality of moral arguments, each of which is rational in terms of its initial premise but which is incompatible with the initial premise of an alternative argument. The abortion debate is an example of incommensurability.

Journalism of attachment: a phrase coined by Martin Bell in opposition to *bystander's journalism*. According to Bell, a journalism of attachment is one which pays heed to demands for objectivity but also recognizes a responsibility to take the side of good against evil, right against wrong, the victim against the oppressor.

Moral: the practices of social actors in the context of the standards (and dominantly in contemporary social and cultural relationships, the feelings) of ethics and of the ethical.

Moral action: the specific form and interpretation of social action (that is, action oriented towards others) which is practised in terms of apprehensions of the right and good or, dominantly in contemporary social and cultural relationships, in terms of feelings of compassion.

Moral voice: Carol Gilligan writes: 'by voice I mean something like what people mean when they speak of the core of the self. Voice is natural and also cultural . . . voice is a powerful psychological instrument and channel, connecting inner and outer worlds . . . This ongoing relational exchange among people is mediated through language and culture, diversity and plurality' (Gilligan 1993: xvi). By this definition, moral voice implies the languages through and by which social actors express their understanding of the relationship between their core self and others. According to Gilligan's work it is possible to identify two dominant moral voices which are gender-focused: the moral voice of justice and fairness (focused among men) and the moral voice of care and attachment (focused among women).

Myth: following Roland Barthes, myth can be defined as the transformation of history into nature. Myth establishes that the different fate of different humans is the result of natural forces and circumstances rather than social and historical factors. By this argument then, famine is always the result of drought or pestilence and rarely the product of war or underdevelopment. Or, more specifically, famine is only the result of war if myth also establishes that this specific country is a place of endemic and irreconcilable ethnic, tribal or religious hatred.

NGOs: non-governmental organizations such as Oxfam or the Red Cross. These organizations are independent of any given nation state and are usually the agencies of humanitarian and other disaster relief efforts. They are also involved in tackling problems of underdevelopment.

Objectivity: the ideal that the media report or representation can reflect with a minimum of subjective bias and distortion an event or situation which has an existence independent of the journalist. This definition, however, refers the discussion back to the distinction which Martin Bell drew between bystander's journalism and the journalism of attachment. What Bell calls bystander's journalism is well suited to the demands of objectivity since it establishes the goal that the journalist should report 'reality' without distortion and without letting her or his subjective (that is, personal) feelings get in the way. Meanwhile, the journalism of attachment can be identified as particularly ill suited to the demands of objectivity since it emphasizes what the journalist feels (that is, it tends towards a privileging of the subjective).

Others: those who are not the individual (the not-I). The constituency of others ranges from one's immediate kith and kin to those who are reported and represented on television or in newspapers. In the latter case, however, the others have lost in a way that immediate kith and kin rarely can, their embodied materiality and solidity as well as their ability to act in relation to and with the individual. Others are oriented towards in social action and, insofar as that orientation is interpreted through and guided by notions of right and wrong or feelings of compassion, they are the concern of moral action.

Report: the provision of information or an account of an event or occurrence. The report is one of the defining productions of the field of journalistic practice. Insofar as the report is shaped by the values or objectivity, then it is likely to take the form of the provision of information. Insofar as the report is shaped by the values of the market and sensationalism, it is likely to take the form of an account. The account will itself tend to emphasize the subjective feelings of the individual journalist.

Representation: for the purposes of this book, 'representation' has meant a likeness or an image. This is a fairly simple definition which brushes aside important epistemological and ontological questions, but it is perfectly sufficient for our purposes. However, 'representation' can also refer to advocacy and political struggle on behalf of others. This latter definition ties the meaning of representation to the dubious notion of civil society.

Sensationalism: a deliberate concern to shock or thrill. In the field of journalistic practice, sensationalism invariably involves an emphasis upon 'human interest'. That journalistic practice which is shaped by the demands of the market is likely to emphasize sensationalism insofar as sensationalism can be guaranteed to secure audiences (and therefore market share which can be delivered to advertisers).

Solidarity: unity and, more ethically, an invariant orientation of social action towards others. Solidarity requires a commitment to the 'us' and the 'we' rather than the 'me'.

Suffering: 'Suffering is the opposite of action. In action, a person freely initiates a series of events in order to bring about some desired state of affairs. In suffering, a person undergoes a series of events initiated from outside and leading to a state of affairs which is not desired' (Macquarrie 1986: 608).

Telethon: a television and/or radio appeal on behalf of a charity or a range of charities. Telethons involve lengthy broadcasts (often of 24 hours) and are invariably aimed at raising funds for specific concerns, e.g. child poverty, famine, flood relief and so forth. Telethon broadcasts are invariably fronted by celebrities and involve the audience engaging in allegedly 'fun' pursuits. Telethons are usually justified on the grounds that, 'it is all in a good cause'.

Universalism: all-inclusiveness. It is possible to talk of *ethical* universalism insofar as a principle can be identified which includes *all* relevant subjects and which refuses to accept limitation according to social or cultural attributes. The subject of universalism is humanity, not any specific nation, 'race', religion or gender. It is possible to talk of *moral* universalism insofar as it is possible to identify social action which is oriented in principle towards all (any and every) others. In these terms, compassion can be identified as a principle and a social action of universalism.

Virtue: the pursuit of the goods that are internal to a practice.

REFERENCES

Alagiah, G. (1998) Contribution to the conference, Dispatches from Disaster Zones: Reporting Humanitarian Disasters, held in London 27–28 May. Transcript available at http: //www.alertnet.org.

Alagiah, G. (1999) New light on the Dark Continent, *The Guardian* (media section), 3 May: 4–5.

Allan, S. (1999) *News Culture*. Buckingham: Open University Press.

Arendt, H. (1973a) *On Revolution*. Harmondsworth: Penguin.

Arendt, H. (1973b) *Men in Dark Times*. Harmondsworth: Penguin.

Aristotle (1980) *The Nicomachean Ethics*. (Trans. D. Ross.) Oxford: Oxford University Press.

Augustine (1997) *On Christian Teaching*. (Trans. R.P.H. Green.) Oxford: Oxford University Press.

Barker, M. and Brooks, K. (1998) On looking into Bourdieu's black box, in R. Dickinson, R. Harindranath and O. Linne (eds) *Approaches to Audiences: A Reader*. London: Arnold.

Barthes, R. (1972) *Mythologies*. (Trans. A. Lavers.) London: Jonathan Cape.

Baudrillard, J. (1994) *The Illusion of the End*. (Trans. C. Turner.) Cambridge: Polity.

Bauman, Z. (1993) *Postmodern Ethics*. Oxford: Blackwell.

Bauman, Z. (1998a) *Globalization: The Human Consequences*. Cambridge: Polity.

Bauman, Z. (1998b) *Work, Consumerism and the New Poor*. Buckingham: Open University Press.

Bell, M. (1996a) *In Harm's Way: Reflections of a War-Zone Thug* (revised edition). Harmondsworth: Penguin.

Bell, M. (1996b) Conflict of interest, *The Guardian*, 11 July: 19.

Bell, M. (1998) The journalism of attachment, in M. Kieran (ed.), *Media Ethics*. London: Routledge.

Bellah, R.N., Madsen, R., Sullivan, W.M., Swidler, A. and Tipton, S.M. (1986)

Habits of the Heart: Individualism and Commitment in American Life. New York: Harper & Row.

Boccardi, L.D. (1995) Let the reporters report, in E.R. Girardet (ed.), *Somalia, Rwanda, and Beyond: The Role of the International Media in Wars and Humanitarian Crises*. Dublin: Crosslines.

Boltanski, L. (1999) *Distant Suffering: Morality, Media and Politics*. (Trans. G. Burchell.) Cambridge: Cambridge University Press.

Bourdieu, P. (1984) *Distinction: A Social Critique of the Judgement of Taste*. (Trans. R. Nice.) Cambridge, Mass: Harvard University Press.

Bourdieu, P. (1998) *On Television and Journalism*. (Trans. P. Parkhurst Ferguson.) London: Pluto.

Carbonell, J.L. and Figley, C.R. (1996) When trauma hits home: personal trauma and the family therapist, *Journal of Marital and Family Therapy*, 22(1): 53–8.

Carroll, N. (1998) Is the medium a (moral) message?, in M. Kieran (ed.), *Media Ethics*. London: Routledge.

Culf, A. (1996) BBC man attacks neutral war reports, *The Guardian*, 23 November: 8.

Cushman, T. and Mestrovic, S.G. (1996) *This Time We Knew: Western Responses to Genocide in Bosnia*. New York: New York University Press.

Devereux, E. (1996) Good causes, God's poor and telethon television, *Media, Culture and Society*, 18: 47–68.

Devereux, E. (1998) *Devils and Angels: Television, Ideology and the Coverage of Poverty*. Luton: University of Luton Press.

di Giovanni, J. (1994) Tired moving of the pictures: Bosnia and Rwanda, *Sunday Times*, 14 August: 10/8.

Douglas, M. (1992) *Risk and Blame: Essays in Cultural Theory*. London: Routledge.

Dowell, W. (1995) Reporting the wars, in E.R. Girardet (ed.), *Somalia, Rwanda, and Beyond: The Role of the International Media in Wars and Humanitarian Crises*. Dublin: Crosslines.

Durkheim, E. (1984) *The Division of Labour in Society*. (Trans. W.D. Halls.) London: Macmillan.

Dyck, E.J. and Coldevin, G. (1992) Using positive vs negative photographs for third-world fund raising, *Journalism Quarterly*, 68(3): 572–9.

Edgar, D. (1985) Why aid came alive, *Marxism Today*, September: 26–30.

Finkielkraut, A. (1998) *The Future of a Negation: Reflections on the Question of Genocide*. (Trans. M. Byrd Kelly.) Lincoln, NB: University of Nebraska Press.

Gilligan, C. (1993) *In a Different Voice: Psychological Theory and Women's Development* (2nd edition). Cambridge, MA: Harvard University Press.

Gilligan, C. and Attanucci, J. (1988) Two moral orientations, in C. Gilligan, J.V. Ward and J. McLean Taylor (eds), *Mapping the Moral Domain: A Contribution of Women's Thinking to Psychological Theory and Education*. Cambridge, MA: Harvard University Press.

Gilligan, C. and Wiggins, G. (1988) The origins of morality in early childhood relationships, in C. Gilligan, J.V. Ward and J. McLean Taylor (eds), *Mapping the Moral Domain: A Contribution of Women's Thinking to Psychological Theory and Education*. Cambridge, MA: Harvard University Press.

Girardet, E.R. (ed.) (1995) *Somalia, Rwanda, and Beyond: The Role of the International Media in Wars and Humanitarian Crises*. Dublin: Crosslines.

Girardet, E.R. (1996) Reporting humanitarianism: are the new electronic media making a difference?, in R.I. Rotberg and T.G. Weiss (eds) *From Massacres to Genocide: The Media, Public Policy, and Humanitarian Crises*. Washington, DC: Brookings Institution and Cambridge, MA: World Peace Foundation.

Green, J. (1991) *Neologisms: New Words since 1960*. London: Bloomsbury.

Hammock, J.C. and Charny, J.R. (1996) Emergency response as morality play: the media, the relief agencies, and the need for capacity building, in R.I. Rotberg and T.G. Weiss (eds) *From Massacres to Genocide: The Media, Public Policy, and Humanitarian Crises*. Washington, DC: Brookings Institution and Cambridge, MA: World Peace Foundation.

Harrison, P. and Palmer, R. (1986) *News Out of Africa: Biafra to Band Aid*. London: Hilary Shipman.

Ignatieff, M. (1998) *The Warrior's Honor: Ethnic War and the Modern Conscience*. London: Chatto and Windus.

Keane, F. (1996) *Letter to Daniel: Despatches from the Heart*. (Ed. T. Grant.) London: BBC/Penguin.

Kieran, M. (1998) Objectivity, impartiality and good journalism, in M. Kieran (ed.), *Media Ethics*. London: Routledge.

Kinnick, K.N., Krugman, D.M. and Cameron, G.T. (1996) Compassion fatigue: communication and burnout toward social problems, *Journalism and Mass Communications Quarterly*, 73(3): 687–707.

Kinsey, J. (1987) Use of children in advertising, *International Journal of Advertising*, 6: 169–77.

Kundera, M. (1984) *The Unbearable Lightness of Being*. (Trans. M.H. Heim.) London: Faber & Faber.

Lewis, H.G. (1983) Don't make the creative mistakes that cut response, *Fund Raising Management*, June: 52–5.

Lubbe, H. (1996) The ethics of media use: media consumption as a moral challenge, in K. Dyson and W. Homolka (eds) *Culture First! Promoting Standards in the New Media Age*. London: Cassell.

MacIntyre, A. (1967) *Secularization and Moral Change*. London: Oxford University Press.

MacIntyre, A. (1985) *After Virtue: A Study in Moral Theory* (2nd edition). London: Duckworth.

Macquarrie, J. (1986) Suffering, in J. Macquarrie and J. Childress (eds), *A New Dictionary of Christian Ethics*. London: SCM Press.

Marshall, T.H. (1977) *Class, Citizenship and Social Development*. Chicago: Chicago University Press.

Marx, K. and Engels, F. (1942) The Communist Manifesto, in *Karl Marx: Selected Works in Two Volumes* (volume 1). London: Lawrence & Wishart.

Mauss, M. (1990) *The Gift: Forms and Functions of Exchange in Archaic Societies.* (Trans. W.D. Halls.) London: Routledge.

Merton, R.K. (1949) *Social Theory and Social Structure.* New York: The Free Press.

Mills, C. Wright (1959) *The Sociological Imagination.* New York: Oxford University Press.

Moeller, S.D. (1999) *Compassion Fatigue: How the Media Sell Disease, Famine, War and Death.* New York: Routledge.

Natsios, A. (1996) Illusions of influence: the CNN effect in complex emergencies, in R.I. Rotberg and T.G. Weiss (eds) *From Massacres to Genocide: The Media, Public Policy, and Humanitarian Crises.* Washington, DC: Brookings Institution and Cambridge, MA: World Peace Foundation.

Poole, R. (1991) *Morality and Modernity.* London: Routledge.

Rather, D. (1995) The United States and Somalia: assessing responsibility for the intervention, in E.R. Girardet (ed.), *Somalia, Rwanda, and Beyond: The Role of the International Media in Wars and Humanitarian Crises.* Dublin: Crosslines.

Riesman, D. (1960) *The Lonely Crowd: A Study of the Changing American Character.* With N. Glazer and R. Denney. New Haven, CT: Yale University Press.

Rojek, C. (1993) *Ways of Escape: Modern Transformations in Leisure and Travel.* London: Macmillan.

Sacks, J. (1995) *Faith in the Future.* London: Darton, Longman and Todd.

Sayer, A. (1999) Bourdieu, Smith and disinterested judgement, *Sociological Review*, 47(3): 403–31.

Schroth, R.A. (1995) But it's really burning: tragedy and the journalistic conscience, *Columbia Journalism Review*, September/October: 43–5.

Shaw, M. (1996) *Civil Society and Media in Global Crises: Representing Distant Violence.* London: Pinter.

Simmel, G. (1950) *The Sociology of Georg Simmel.* (Ed. and trans. K.H. Wolff.) New York: The Free Press.

Simmel, G. (1997) *Simmel on Culture: Selected Writings.* (Ed. D. Frisby and M. Featherstone.) London: Sage.

Simpson, A. (1985) Charity begins at home, *Ten: 8*, 19: 21–6.

Standley, J. (1998) Contribution to 'Workshop A: Zaire 1996–97: dilemmas and lessons', at the international conference, Dispatches from Disaster Zones: Reporting Humanitarian Disasters, London, 27–28 May. Transcript available at http: //www.alertnet.org.

Stone, J. (2000) *Losing Perspective.* London: International Broadcasting Trust.

Stout, J. (1988) *Ethics after Babel: The Languages of Morals and their Discontents.* Cambridge: James Clark.

Sznaider, N. (1998) The sociology of compassion: a study in the sociology of morals, *Cultural Values*, 2(1): 117–39.

Taylor, J. (1998) *Body Horror: Photojournalism, Catastrophe and War.* Manchester: Manchester University Press.

Tester, K. (1992) *Civil Society*. London: Routledge.

Tester, K. (1997) *Moral Culture*. London: Sage.

Tester, K. (1999a) Emotivism and Bosnia: a note on Giddensian sociology, *Sociological Imagination*, 36(2/3): 154–66.

Tester, K. (1999b) Social theory and morality, *Portsmouth Lecture Series*, Portsmouth, University of Portsmouth.

Vulliamy, E. (1994) *Seasons in Hell: Understanding Bosnia's War*. London: Simon & Schuster.

Vulliamy, E. (1997) Being there, *The Guardian* (review section), 9 May: 2–3 and 22.

Weber, M. (1948) *From Max Weber: Essays in Sociology*. (Ed. and trans. H.H. Gerth and C. Wright Mills.) London: Routledge & Kegan Paul.

Weber, M. (1968) *Economy and Society: An Outline of Interpretive Sociology* (volume 1). (Ed. G. Roth and C. Wittich.) New York: Bedminster Press.

Worsthorne, P. (1999) The art of news, *Prospect*, November: 3–33.

INDEX